FINDING FUNDS FOR YOUR
FILM OR TV PROJECT

FINDING FUNDS
FOR YOUR FILM
OR TV PROJECT

The Most Effective Strategies to Use
for Different Types of Films and Budgets

GINI GRAHAM SCOTT

AN IMPRINT OF HAL LEONARD CORPORATION

Published in 2013 by Limelight Editions
An Imprint of Hal Leonard Corporation
7777 West Bluemound Road
Milwaukee, WI 53213

Trade Book Division Editorial Offices
33 Plymouth St., Montclair, NJ 07042

Printed in the United States of America
Book design by Mark Lerner
Library of Congress Cataloging-in-Publication Data is available upon
request.

ISBN 978-0-87910-878-6

www.limelighteditions.com

Contents

Acknowledgments

I'd like to extend my thanks to the many people in the film community in the San Francisco Bay Area and L.A. who encouraged me to write this book. They also raised many questions that helped guide me in deciding what to include.

Introduction

Finding funds for films involves a series of phases in which you decide what film you are producing; have a completed script; determine how much you need to produce it for the lowest possible budget and with an expanded budget; create the necessary materials to obtain the funds, which may include a business plan, private placement memorandum (PPM), and crowdfunding prospectus; and set up the necessary legal structure to receive those funds, which is often a separate LLC (limited liability corporation) for each film.

You may also need other kinds of documents to show you have the necessary commitments from actors and the top crew members and to show you have the team in place to make the film once you get the necessary funding. The actors may not matter for a low-budget film, but the budget, as well as the interest of distributors, can increase substantially if you do get actors with a name. But normally you need at least the major participants on the team: the writer, producer, director, and director of photography (the last two are sometimes one in the same). At this point you may also include any associate producers, executive producers (who usually contribute funds), and cinematographers.

Other materials to prepare to get funding include flyers and promotional materials to show distributors, producers, and investors, as well as marketing materials to promote your film through social and traditional media and to your personal contacts.

Then, once you have the necessary documents and materials prepared, you are ready for the next phase of finding funds: announcing, presenting, and promoting your project, while keeping in mind the legal limitations on what you can do when asking contributors for money. For example, if you're seeking investors, you normally need to limit your offering to private qualified parties in order to conform to Securities and Exchange Commission (SEC) requirements. Or if you're using a crowdfunding approach, you can offer rewards in return for contributions, but you can't ask for investments or promise a return. Should you approach family and friends, you have much more flexibility in what you say or do, although you should put all promises and expectations in writing to keep things professional and to preserve your relationships if the film loses money—or makes a lot!

This phase typically involves a lot of outreach, which means finding whom to approach and how, what to say in your letters and initial phone calls, and how to network to prospect for leads. Then, once you identify interested individuals or groups, you have to make one-on-one and group presentations, and you have to know how to follow up afterwards to close the deal.

Finally, you need to set up the appropriate banking and escrow arrangements to receive the funds so that you can properly disburse them yourself or with the assistance of a line producer, financial officer, or administrative assistant. For example, you might set up an LLC for your film with its own bank account. This way, you can keep track of what you pay out, keep on top of your expenses and stay on budget, and complete your film.

This book covers each of the major phases, from deciding what you want to film and choosing the script, through finding a team and crafting a budget, to reaching out to investors and contributors, so you have a realistic start to finding the funds you need:

Chapter 1, "Getting Started," focuses on deciding what you want to produce, optioning an already written property or writing the script, preparing a synopsis, determining the cast and crew you need, and coming up with a rough estimate of a high and low budget.

Chapter 2, "Putting Together Information for Investors," covers the major documents you need for different types of funding, which include a budget and schedule, business plan, private placement memorandum (PPM), and necessary legal documents.

Chapter 3, "Creating a Crowdfunding Campaign," deals with how to put on a crowdfunding campaign where you appeal for donations, rather than investments. It discusses the elements of a successful campaign using Kickstarter, Indiegogo, and RocketHub.

Chapter 4, "Marketing, Presenting, and Promoting Your Project," focuses on how to sell contributors or investors on your project, as well as how to find and then contact prospective investors and contributors both in person and online. There's also information on pitching your project to the media and building your credibility and increasing interest in your project by engaging with the film community.

Chapter 5, "Closing the Deal and Getting Your Funds," focuses on how to follow up with leads, negotiate arrangements, close the deal, and complete any necessary paperwork, as well as how to set up a bank and escrow account for your money, so you can then use it for disbursing your funds once you get into production.

Finally, lists of resources and references offer books, websites, film finance organizations, and other information you'll find helpful as you find your funds.

CHAPTER 1

Getting Started

Deciding What to Produce

Deciding what to produce usually starts with a writer, producer, or director becoming intrigued or inspired by a particular idea—a newsworthy event, a personal story of courage or achievement, an article or book, or an earlier film ripe for a remake.

Whatever it is, you'll need to put together a package including a script or treatment, synopsis, and analysis of the projected budget, and a list of the cast and crew needed under various high to low budget scenarios. In selecting a property, consider whether it will be practical in light of production needs and how to scale it to produce it for different budget levels. And because the timeline from inception to completing a feature film or documentary can vary greatly, from a few months to a few years or more, you'll have to determine whether you have the time and energy to commit to the project.

Considering the Market Opportunities

In selecting a property for development, remember your initial inspiration or idea, and review film industry trends and the markets that will be most interested in your type of film. Consider what else is already out there on your subject. Is there an expanding level of interest in this topic, or is the market saturated? How can you make your film stand out from the competition? Also, think about whether the film is too timely (such as a film tied to current event), or whether there still will be interest in this topic in the few years it takes to fund and complete the film. Likewise, think of the market for your film. Is it for a general or niche audience? Will it appeal most to certain age, sex, ethnic, or other groups? Does the potential market appeal justify the production budget?

These are all questions to ask yourself in deciding on what to produce, as these are also questions to answer in writing your business plan and pitching your project to potential investors and contributors. They will want to see not only that your proposed budget is realistic but also that the film is likely to make money.

Preparing a Script and/or Treatment

Once you decide on the property to develop and seek funds for, the next step is getting a script and/or treatment, which you can obtain in one of three ways: write it yourself, hire a writer, or secure the rights to an already completed script or book. Investors and contributors will want to know that you have full rights to this property when they are investing or contributing funds.

Writing It Yourself

Even if you write the script or treatment yourself, include the payment to yourself as part of the budget. There are several ways to do this:

- Pay yourself the full amount for the script based on common industry standards for a script of that length for that type of film—for example, $5,000–$10,000 for a low-budget film script from a new scriptwriter. Experienced scriptwriters will often be paid more, say $15,000–$25,000. However, these amounts are far below the payments expected by WGA (Writers Guild of America) writers, where the minimum is $70,000, but for a low-budget indie feature or documentary, the lower figures are much more typical.
- Pay yourself a percentage of the budget raised for shooting the film. Typically, this percentage is around 3%, which would be $1,500 for a film with a $50,000 budget, or $3,000 for a film with a $100,000 budget.
- Pay yourself an initial fee or percentage of the budget; then, you get an additional fee or percentage based on

the film's gross or net income from any sources, with the initial fee or percentage considered an advance against royalties.

Whichever approach you use, include it in the "above-the-line" budget section, which includes what is paid to any writers, directors, and producers of the film.

Hiring a Writer

Hiring a writer is a common practice in the film industry when a producer, writer, or director has an idea for a film, an outline with major plot points, or even a novel or memoir to be adapted into a script, but doesn't have the time or ability to write a script. You can work with a writer or a ghostwriter, depending on whether the writer is getting credited.

Look for a writer by listing a writing job with writing or screenwriting groups, such as the American Society of Journalists and Authors or the L.A. Screenwriters, or post an ad on Craigslist for your location and elsewhere. Also, use business networking groups and personal and professional referrals.

Generally, if you haven't secured your funding, you'll have to advance the funds to pay the writer yourself or work out a percentage or reduced fee and percentage arrangement. Normally, established professional writers will not work for a percentage only, because they make their living by writing and rarely or never take scripts on spec for clients. However, many will give you a reduced rate or accept a partial payment up front with the rest deferred until after funding in return for a percentage of the film's earnings. While less-experienced writers may be willing to take a chance on a spec script, most won't—so expect to pay something, with the amount dependent on the writer's experience and willingness to work on a percentage or deferred basis. Determine how much you can pay out of pocket to help you decide on the best arrangement with the writer.

However you do it, there are four key considerations for hiring a writer, the last three of which will become part of the package for potential investors.

1. Find an experienced writer who is right for the particular job at the price you can pay.

   However you find a writer, check out his or her experience, references, and availability to determine whether he or she will be a good fit for your planned project. Ask the writer to submit a sample script or excerpts, ideally in the genre of your film, or at least in a related genre (such as mystery/thriller if you are doing crime action adventure). If instead you ask prospective writers to submit new pages based on your idea, have them first fill out nondisclosure agreements (NDAs), in which they promise to not use any of your material in their own writing or show it to others—and also expect to pay them for their work.

Additionally, consider how well you feel you can work with this writer. He or she should be able to provide ideas and suggestions; at the same time, he or she should recognize that you are in charge and should be willing to write the script—and rewrite it—the way you want.

Finally, determine what the writer expects to be paid and whether this fits your budget, or be up-front about your budget so you know that the writers contacting you are willing to work within it.

2. Secure the rights and payment arrangements by contract.

With any writer, start with a work-for-hire agreement, so you own and control all of the rights, unless the writer adds a substantial amount of original material (more than 50% of the script) as you go along, in which case it makes sense to share the rights and become partners. Write up any agreements so any such determination is up to you, so there's no question about ownership of the property, which you need to get funding.

Likewise, spell out the payment arrangements. Common arrangements including having an agreement for the full price for the project, based on an estimated number of pages, and then staggering the payments; and

having a pay-as-you-go-project, based on an initial re-
tainer and followed by additional payments, paid on a
per-word, per-page, or hourly basis, to the completion
of the project.

3. Get an NDA to protect your property.

The NDA (non-disclosure agreement) is designed to
be signed by the writer before you show him or her anything about the project; its purpose is to make it clear
that you don't want the writer to discuss anything about
your project with anyone. The NDA shows investors that
you are serious about your project and puts the writer
on notice that you want to protect your idea.

4. Get a copyright in your name or have the copyright
    assigned to you.

The agreement to hire a writer should include a clause
that you or your company as the author is the owner of
the work, such as "The Author will own the Work, including any copyrights and sale or distribution rights,"
or the writer is "transferring or assigning any rights in
the work" to you. However the agreement is written—
and even if you've written the script yourself—consider
registering the script with the WGA (Writers Guild of
America), and register the copyright for the property
with the US Copyright Office. This acts as a deterrent to

any copying, and investors will want to see that you have this copyright registration in your name, which is part of the "chain of title" requirement to show that there's a clear title and that you have full rights to the property you plan to produce.

Securing the Rights to a Script or Book

To secure film rights to produce an already written script—and to get funding, a bank loan, and insurance—you need an agreement from the author or current property owner.

Consider starting with an option, which is much less expensive than licensing or purchasing rights to the property; this gives you a specified period of time in which you have the exclusive right to exercise the option. If you choose to exercise it, you can license or purchase the property, or if you need more time to secure a license or make a purchase, you can ask to extend the option. In fact, some agreements have a built-in extension clause. The purpose of the option period, which typically lasts from 3 months to a year, unless extended, is to give you the opportunity to raise funds based on having this exclusive option on the property. Once funding is in place or is likely, you can exercise the option by paying the specified licensing fee or purchase price.

The cost of the option can range from a nominal amount—even as little as $1 offered in consideration—to $25,000. If a script is purchased, common amounts are

$2,500 to $10,000 for a complete buy-out, often less if the writer has the opportunity for additional income after the script sells, but a highly desirable property may command $200,000–$500,000, or even more. These costs of options and licensing fees are based on the value of the property. If the script is for a project that already has a brand name, is by an established author, or is based on a bestselling book, the value will be much more, so the option fee and licensing fee will be much higher. On the other hand, if you are making a low-budget feature, you'll probably be acquiring the rights to a property that hasn't proven itself yet in the marketplace and is by a less-established writer, so you can expect to pay much less. You can pay even less if you offer the writer or property owner a share of the backend profits, which may prove even more profitable in the long run if the film does well.

Establishing the Chain of Title

As soon as you have someone else write your script or you select a book, article, script, or idea provided by someone else, you need to have the necessary documents establishing your ownership. You have to establish this before making your movie, or you won't be able to get your funds released, the insurance you need, or even a distribution deal. You also need to make sure there are no breaks in the chain if you pick up a property previously owned by

someone else. Chain of title documents are also required
by banks for any films they decide to finance, and investors commonly want to know you have these, too. The
chain of title documents may vary depending on the type
of underlying rights, and they may include any or all of
the following:

- Option Agreement, which must be in writing and must
  be signed by the person who owns the copyright in the
  underlying work (short form version available). Provisions include the following:
    - Parties to the Agreement (whoever owns the rights
      to the property)
    - Consideration for the Option (payment for the
      option)
    - Option Period (length of time the option will last)
    - Exercise of Option (how the producer will exercise
      the option and payment arrangements)
    - Assignment (property rights are assignable to the
      producer, and the producer will have the right to
      assign the property to others)
    - Entire Agreement Clause (the agreement represents
      the complete understanding between the parties
      and supersedes any other agreements; the agree-
      ment cannot be modified except in writing and
      must be signed by both parties)

- Governing Law (which country's or state's laws govern the agreement; where the disputes will be sub-
  mitted to arbitration or adjudication)

- Option Extension Agreement, which is necessary if the
  time period for the original option has run out; includes
  the same provisions as above.

- Assignment or Purchase Agreement, which can be en-
  tered into directly or once whoever has an option agreement chooses to exercise that option (short form version
  available). Provisions include the following:

  - Parties to the Agreement (whoever owns the rights
    to the property)
  - Rights Granted (exactly what rights are being
    acquired)
  - Duration and Extent of Rights Granted (how long
    the producer can develop the underlying rights)
  - Right to Make Changes (producer may alter and
    adapt the underlying work)
  - Consideration (full payment for the acquisition of
    the rights)
  - Representation and Warranties and No Infringe-
    ment (ownership and originality)
  - Indemnity (each party indemnifies and holds harm-
    less any other parties)
  - Credit Provisions (parties will receive the agreed-
    upon credit in the film)

- • Assignment (producer has the right to transfer or assign the agreement)
- • Assignment of Copyright
- • Quit Claim
- • Writer's Agreement
- • Publisher's Release
- • Life Story Rights Agreement

In some cases, if required by the bank and other financiers, the producer's lawyer may additionally need to provide a chain of title opinion, based on reviewing all of the underlying rights documents and stating that the producer has, and can assign, all rights needed for the film. The reason for the lawyer's opinion is to get an additional reassurance that all of the underlying rights are properly under the producer's control, so there's no likelihood of potential litigation or a claim made against the film.

Preparing a Log Line and Synopsis

Creating a compelling log line and synopsis is also necessary for introducing prospective contributors and investors to your project, before they look at the script, fundraising documents, or business plan more closely. The log line and synopsis can become important parts of your marketing and promotional materials, and in developing them, it's a good idea to test out your materials on other writers and producers to help you refine and polish them so you'll make a powerful presentation.

The log line is a stand-alone pitch of about 25–50 words or about 140–200 characters, which is designed to grab the reader and make him or her want to know more. A synopsis is a slightly longer description and summary of the film, which can take various forms:

- A short description of the project, which is typically a log line summarizing the script in 25–50 words followed by a short paragraph featuring the main highlights of the film and why it will appeal to an audience and to contributors or investors.
- A 1-page synopsis, which typically starts with the 25- to 50-word log line and then includes several paragraphs describing the main plot points, as well as a brief description of the writer or company producing the project.
- A more extensive 3- to 20-page treatment, which is essentially an expanded synopsis that describes in more detail what happens in the story, much like a comprehensive outline, and might also include information about the writer or company producing the project.

Examples of a log line and several different synopses of different lengths developed for a film called *The Suicide*

Party, which as of this writing is being pitched to investors by Changemakers Productions, can be found in the Appendix.

Determining the Needed Cast and Crew

Even before you do a detailed breakdown for the schedule and budget, you need a general sense of the key cast and crew members required to produce the film. Later, when it's time to create the budget, you can factor in the smaller roles for supporting cast and extras, as well as for the supporting crew members, since they are easily recruited wherever you are filming. However, you want to determine the main players so you can include them in your pitch for funding. In fact, laying out these details can help you recruit principal cast members and crew, which you'll then use in seeking contributors and investors.

Sketching out a rough idea of the needed cast and crew can also help you determine your budget and assess whether your initial planning to produce this project is realistic for the anticipated budget or whether you'll need more money. Or alternatively, you might scale down the scope of your project, such as by reducing the number of principal players and crew members. For much of this early planning, you have to be able to adapt, since so many elements go into producing a successful film and getting funds for it, and adjusting the needed cast and crew is a critical part of this process.

Creating Your Cast List

To create your cast list, go through the script and pull out the most important characters, including the leads and the supporting actors who have significant roles with at least several pages of dialogue. Then, write up short 1- to 2-sentence descriptions for each character, including the character's age range, occupation or role in the story, and the main things the character does in furthering the action.

Once you have this character list, you can more easily let actors and casting directors know who will be the principal players, and this list can help you bring in an established casting director, should you want one, as well as name actors, who can see themselves in a particular role. In turn, if you get an interested actor with a name, this can immediately increase your film's appeal to distributors and sales agents, and as a result to contributors and funders. Your budget may need to be increased at this point to cover the higher salary expected by a name actor, but that can increase your film's returns, although many name actors will work for scale—the SAG minimum of $100 a day for a low-budget film under $250,000—commonly in return for a piece of the backend after the success of the picture.

After listing all of the leads and major supporting characters, many producers also create what is known as a "wish list," in which they list the name actors they might like to see in each role if they could choose whomever they wanted.

Even if your ideal cast is out of reach, the wish list can help you in casting the film, even with unknowns, since you'll be looking for someone with the characteristics of those on your list for each role—and this will also help guide a casting director in the appropriate direction. In some cases, if you can get your script to one of the actors on your wish list, you may even get that actor to be in your film. Even if you can't get the name actors for your project, creating the list will help you think about what types of people you want in different parts.

It's also helpful to line up actors for the key roles in the film. You can use a casting service, such as SF Casting in the San Francisco or East Bay area, L.A. Casting in Los Angeles, or a casting director who handles actors in your area, to help you choose some likely actors for different roles. If you're creating a trailer or sizzle reel and later get funding, you can include the same actor in the feature film, although sometimes a trailer or sizzle reel is just used to illustrate and pitch the feature film. Then, you do your casting for the film separately.

Getting Letters of Intent

Once you are casting for the film, get a letter of intent that the person is willing to be in that part, subject to his or her availability at the time of shooting. For big-budget films, often an agreement to get an actor to commit to a film is a pay-or-play agreement; in low-budget films, these agreements tend to be more informal. You can use letters of intent when you pitch the film to investors or to contributors for a crowd-funding campaign. An example of a letter of intent used in developing and pitching *The Parking Lot* can be found in the Appendix.

Besides having the letter of intent, also include information on each actor (e.g., bio, photo, list of credits, links to an online reel, sample clips). This way, the contributor or investor can see the actors you are proposing to include in your film. Even if you have to make last-minute changes due to an actor's unavailability at the time of the shoot, this will still show the level of experience of those actors currently committed to the project.

Determining the Key Crew Members

Unless you can get one or more name actors attached (although this is unlikely with a new producer and low-budget production), your most important team members to get financing will be your crew members. Include bios of each individual, along with links to their past work, recommendations, or websites. The key crew members to include in your proposal for funding are the following:

- the director, who will sometimes be the same as the director of photography (DP);
- the DP, sometimes called the cinematographer;

- a second cinematographer or 2nd camera;
- a casting director (if you have one with an extensive background in the industry); and
- the editor.

It's especially important to select as your director and cinematographer individuals with at least several years' experience who have examples of their work in a reel online or in links to works by other producers. Preferably, choose a director and cinematographer who have done feature films before; but if they have done great work in shorter films, that still can impress contributors and investors.

If you have other crew members, such as a production manager or line producer, who are playing a significant role and have extensive experience, you can include them, too; otherwise, leave them out.

Other key players to mention, if you have people with extensive experience, include an associate producer, co-director, publicist or PR company, and marketing director. Should you already have any commitments of funds, list those people in the proposal as executive producers.

Obtain letters of intent from your top crew members, too, so you—and your contributors and investors—know they are committed to the project if you obtain funding. A sample letter of intent for a director for *The Parking Lot* project can be found in the Appendix.

Coming Up with a Rough Estimate of Your Budget

You'll need a much more detailed and accurate budget when you follow up with your investors and contributors who want more information before giving you money. But initially, to prepare your introductory materials for when you first approach prospective investors, contributors, and others to participate in your film, you need a general idea of what your budget will be. Consider budgeting your film into different phases for funding: Phase I, to make the film; Phase II, to market, distribute, and promote it.

It's helpful to make a distinction between completing the film and seeking to make money with it, because often once a film is produced, you can get more money from investors and contributors to distribute and promote the film, as well as payments from distributors, networks, and others who want to buy or license distribution rights. Thus, the figure to use for the rough estimate of your budget is the amount to produce a completed film, although you need to note if you plan to have anyone work on a deferred pay basis, along with any payments to investors, before the film can start making a profit.

The key factors to consider for this preliminary budget are the number of scenes and locations, the size of the cast and crew, and the number of shooting days. Individuals who specialize in creating budgets have to first break down the script into scenes and determine what scenes to shoot when based on the actors needed and their availability, so that they can factor in all of the costs for actors, crew members, location, equipment, craft services to feed the cast and crew, props, and other materials needed for the production. For now, just do a rough estimate based on all these elements, and if needed, consider ways to reduce the number of locations, scenes, and actors to cut down your costs.

Alternatively, figure on adjusting the script to meet a certain budget, such as aiming for a $40,000–$50,000 budgeted film. Figure on the lowest budget you need to make the film and the full budget needed to do the film the way you want to do it.

You can keep these initial budget figures down if you have people willing to work for a small amount down and on a deferred basis. However, don't try to get everyone to agree to defer everything, because you generally need some up-front payment to ensure that people will be, and can afford to be, committed for a shoot lasting two or more weeks. Once there's some money in the mix, many cast and crew members will agree to work for this low amount, since they believe in the project and expect to be well rewarded for their participation in the end.

CHAPTER 2

Putting Together Information for Investors

Depending on the type of funding you're seeking, you'll need a number of different documents. These are in addition to the copyright, option, assignment, purchase, and chain of title opinion already described to ensure your rights to the property and to convince prospective investors and contributors to support your project, as well as any marketing and promotional materials, which you'll need to announce and promote your offering.

These key documents include the following, and you should create those that you'll need for your type of project:

- An organizational structure, usually an LLC for each film, unless you want to set up a structure for a series of films or for your whole company.
- A budget and schedule, which breaks down your script according to filming days, locations, actors, crew, props, and costs, so you know what you need for the shoot.
- A business plan, which includes a complete budget and schedule or a summary, along with details on the project;

the management team; the cast and crew to date; comparables on the marketplace; the amount of money needed; plans for production, distribution, and promotion; and the return on investment.

- A private placement memorandum (PPM), which specifies the terms of the investment, along with the return projected under low, medium, and high scenarios.

- A crowdfunding prospectus, posted on a crowdfunding site such as Indiegogo, Kickstarter, or RocketHub, which describes the project, entices site visitors to contribute, and indicates the rewards offered as an incentive to contribute different levels of funds, from $1 or $2 to several thousand dollars.

Creating an Organizational Structure

You'll need some kind of organizational structure to receive any funds. The type of structure to set up depends on where you are in the funding process (e.g., seeking funds to develop the film and set up the corporation), your expected relationship with the funders (i.e., whether they are active or passive participants or a combination of these), and whether you'll primarily get your funding from one or a few investors or a great many passive investors. In the event that you use crowdfunding for any or all of your funds, these will be contributors, not investors, and you can use any of these structures, as well as receive funds as a private party.

The major types of organizational structures to set up are the following active and passive investor vehicles. Those with active investors aren't considered securities, so they don't trigger SEC regulations as those with passive investors do, unless you meet various exemptions. In most cases, it's best to see an attorney to help you set up the appropriate vehicle and file the necessary papers in your state, typically with the secretary of state, as well as with the city or county in which you're operating. A chart outlining the different types of structures for different types of funding can be found in the Appendix.

The Active Investor Vehicles

In active investor vehicles, the investors play an active part in the organization's operations, though this activity can range from participating in day-to-day management to attending occasional board meetings and providing input on operations from a distance. This type of organization can be an ideal vehicle for bringing in a small amount of capital—say, less than $50,000—for an independent film, where you can contribute some of your own funds, such as from savings, credit cards, or a bank loan; this structure also works well if you can round up funds from a small number of people you know, including family, friends, and some wealthy individuals who are inspired by the subject of your feature or documentary.

Such a structure can be much less complicated than other investment vehicles, and you can easily set it up under contract law, specifying who does what and who receives what if the film makes a profit. But the downside of this structure is the liability of all the active investors if things go wrong, although in the contract you can specify that the investor is only providing you with funds and has no liability. In that case, the investor is really being a passive investor, but is exempt from SEC regulations, since you are making a private offering.

The common way to obtain funds through this structure is with an investor-financing agreement in which you provide the investor with a business plan or other statement describing what you plan to do with the funds and the expected return on investment. This agreement is basically a contract between you as the producer or the production company and the investor. Once the investor signs the contract with you and hands you a check, you have the funds for the company, film, initial incorporation, or whatever the agreement specifies.

These are the five main vehicles in this category.

The Sole Proprietorship

The sole proprietorship is often the first business structure you might set up when starting to produce and fund your first film, commonly by using your own funds or by obtaining funds from friends and family as a loan or gift. With such a structure, you need to file for an assumed or fictitious name, which creates a "DBA" or "doing business as" name. If your company has different divisions, or if you simply want to use alternate names, you can file for additional names for just a small charge.

Once your fictitious name is on file, you can open up a bank account, and you can gain recognition as a local business in your city by registering as a business and paying a small tax. Go to the Recorder's Office in your city hall to find out what to do in your city.

Creating a sole proprietorship with a DBA has various advantages:

- Obtaining gifts, grants, loans, and a limited number of investments using an investor-financing agreement.
- Serving in various capacities in other structures in order to raise funds to develop, produce, and distribute the film under this other entity.
- Retaining creative control.
- Avoiding having to engage in any formal meetings or keep records of these meetings or of board votes, as in a corporation.

- Being taxed at a lower rate as a sole proprietor.

  There are also disadvantages to a sole proprietorship:

- Covering the initial start-up costs before you get outside funding.
- Finding it more difficult to get funds from investors as a sole proprietor.
- Being personally liable for any obligations or debts incurred by the company.
- Finding that many businesses would rather do business with a corporation than with a sole proprietorship.
- Getting key employees to work for you or participate in profit-sharing or a deferred payment arrangement.

Still, despite such disadvantages, the sole proprietorship might be a good way to get started while you set up another structure for raising additional funding.

General Partnership

In a general partnership, you team up with one or more other people to carry out any business activity (e.g., producing a particular film or establishing a film production company) and having a continuing business relationship. Have a written agreement that states what each partner is expected to do in return for what share of the earnings. Any laws governing partnerships are established by each state, although typically in a partnership, the partners:

- express a desire to be partners and contribute money, property, or their skills and time to the business;
- share in the control of the business;
- receive a share of any profits; and
- share in any of the business's losses or liabilities.

A general partnership provides several advantages:

- It can be a good way to raise a limited amount of start-up capital when people are first going into business together and haven't yet created another structure to organize their business.
- Any new partners won't be personally liable for any actions or omissions that occurred before they joined the partnership. This is important for providing new partners with the security of knowing that they won't take on any past liabilities when they join the partnership.
- It can be used as a film production or operating company in a limited partnership (LP) or can act as the manager of a manager-managed LLC, where the LP or LLC are the investment vehicles.

At the same time, there are some disadvantages of a general partnership:

- All the partners are liable for the partnership's debts and obligations.
- It's generally not a good vehicle for raising significant amounts of capital, because the partners have unlimited liability and can't freely transfer their interests, and the partnership has a decentralized management structure.

As long as all partners take an active role in the partnership, such an arrangement is not considered a security. But if certain partners don't actively participate in management while expecting a return on their investment, such as when a film producer seeks funds from a large group of investors, your company is really operating as a limited partnership selling unregistered securities, although there are exemptions when a small number of qualified investors participate in a private placement. Thus, if you start with a general partnership and gain more than a few interested investors, change to another business structure to receive these funds.

Joint Venture

A joint venture is a more specialized type of general partnership, that is created for a limited purpose, such as producing a single feature film or putting together a TV or web series.

In a joint venture, all the investors must not only be few in number and financially knowledgeable, but they must also be active in some way, such as coming to the set or reviewing daily rushes with the editor and director. If they are not active, the joint venture has become a limited partnership.

Commonly, when you are seeking funding for a film, a joint venture is composed of two or more companies that contribute different elements to the film (e.g., contributing some or all of the money, contributing the script or underlying property, taking the lead in putting together the cast and crew, contributing locations or leading the search for alternate locations). In some cases, these joint ventures, as well as general partnerships, are set up between corporations, so the owners of these companies enjoy the limited liability protections offered by their corporations, even though the joint venture itself offers no such protection.

Generally, in setting up a joint venture, it's good to work out arrangements in advance about who is responsible for what, including who has creative control and how much influence the various parties to the venture will have, including whether they will have the right of approval for the final cut and what kind of film credit they will receive. Also include various property rights (e.g., licensing), how profits and losses will be allocated, how disputes might be resolved, the duration of the joint venture, and the agreement's termination or renewal date. Having such terms spelled out will make it clear who own what rights or owns which rights and will also contribute to maintaining the chain of title.

The advantages of a joint venture include the following:

- There's no needed to comply with detailed federal and state security laws because it isn't considered a security.
- The agreement is also shorter and less complicated than setting up a limited partnership, LLC, or corporation, and you don't need to file papers with the secretary of state.

The main disadvantage of a joint venture is the following:

- Partners need to be active in the project; as a result, disputes might arise over creative decisions, but those can be worked out by setting out provisions about who makes the decision in the event of a dispute.

Initial Incorporation

Another way to obtain a limited amount of funds—particularly if you've already gotten some interest but don't want to fund the whole project yourself—is to create a new corporation to start the fundraising and production process. Commonly, this kind of corporate structure is created when a producer brings together a few friends, family members, or business associates who contribute cash, property, or past services in return for shares in the company; they become founding shareholders in a new corporation.

Initial incorporation advantages include the following:

- You won't have to sell shares in a corporation, per SEC regulations, because of a private investment exemption.
- It can be part of a two-stage investor solicitation strategy (the second stage involves searching for funds from new shareholder investors, which is considered a securities offering that must be registered with the SEC and with state securities regulators).
- It allows you to go after angel capital, commonly from individual wealthy investors who provide early-stage financing.

The disadvantages of initial incorporation include the following:

- The amount of money you are seeking for an indie feature or documentary may be too small for an individual venture capitalist to consider.
- You may end up in a conflict over creative issues, such as your choice of a director, the director's vision of the film, and the talent you want to cast for lead roles, with

your investors and shareholders—which could result in you being outvoted, or even fired!

Consider such an initial corporation as just an initial vehicle for bringing in early capital; then, look at different organizational structures for the long term.

Member-Managed LLC

A member-managed LLC combines elements of a corporation, limited partnership, and general partnership. With this member-managed setup, a limited number of investors actively manage the company with you in a more democratic fashion, based on management by committee and majority vote. Since all are active, this type of LLC does not trigger any sale or offer of security laws.

The advantages of a member-managed LLC include the following:

- You have the limited liability benefits of a corporation and the tax benefits of a partnership.
- Member-managed LLCs are also more flexible and informal to operate.
- You can use this structure for company operations, as well as for bringing in first-level financing to get the company off the ground.

The disadvantages of a member-managed LLC are the following:

- This structure is not designed to bring in a large amount of financing from a large number of investors.
- A more democratic decision-making process means possible creative control problems should investors have different ideas about what the company should do or how a particular film should be produced.
- The LLC is subject to an annual franchise tax, like a corporation, in most states, and many states may apply a gross receipts tax.

On the balance, the member-managed LLC can be a good alternative to a partnership when bringing in funds from a small number of investors.

The Passive Investor Vehicles

The most common way to bring in funds from a large number of investors is through one of the passive investor vehicles, but such vehicles do trigger SEC considerations—however, if you limit these organizations to fewer than 20 investors who meet a financial threshold and you obtain them through private contacts and referrals, rather than through advertising for investors, you can be exempt from registering your offering as a security. Consider hiring an attorney who specializes in setting up corporations, and check with the current laws and filing arrangements in your state to be sure you have the latest information.

The Manager-Managed LLC

The manager-managed LLC, which is most commonly referred to as simply an "LLC," is one of the most popular vehicles used for raising funds for films, and typically a single LLC is created for each film.

The advantages of an LLC include the following:

- Everyone has limited liability protection, and it becomes the operating unit for receiving and disbursing funds.
- It can be used to raise funds quickly as a private offering to qualified investors with whom you have a pre-existing relationship (i.e., with people you have personally met).
- You can create one after you have the interested investors ready to invest by selling what are called "pre-formation units." This way, you don't spend the time and effort to create the LLC, which can cost about $1,500 to $2,000 if an attorney creates one for you.
- You have full creative control and don't have to get the approval of a board of directors or investor-members, as long as you operate as described in the LLC's operating rules.

The disadvantages of an LLC include the following:

- You need an operating agreement, which is approved and signed by the members, and these operating rules are longer and more complex than those in the member-managed LLC.
- You need to specify detailed rules in advance, whereas in a member-managed LLC, the members can make up and approve new rules as you go along.
- You have to comply with federal and state securities laws, because the investors receive units or interests in the LLC, which are considered securities.
- If you do make significant changes to your initial project, you may need to get the approval of investor-members, as provided for in the LLC's operating agreement.
- SEC rules specify how many investors you can seek out and under what conditions, and some states have stricter rules—so check them out yourself or work with an attorney experienced in such filings.

Limited Partnership

In a limited partnership (LP), one or more general partners run the company, with other limited partners who are simply investors. All of the partners must sign the partnership agreement, as well as a certificate of limited partnership, which is filed with the secretary of state where the partnership is formed. You can offer a certain number of units in the limited partnership, which will be formed when it gets funded, but these units are considered securities.

While the general partners manage the company, most or all of the money commonly comes from the limited partners, and they cannot be involved in management or they lose their limited partner status, including their protection from liabilities. But as long as they remain limited partners, the most they can lose is their investment.

The advantages of an LP are the following:

- You can operate the company freely, as long as you comply with the partnership agreement and the state laws affecting a partnership.
- It's an ideal structure for financing single pictures or a slate of pictures, because it's for a limited term and there are no taxes on it as an entity.
- It costs less to maintain than a corporation does, as it requires fewer meetings and no minutes. It offers more creative control.

The disadvantage of an LP is the following:

- You have to register LPs with the federal and state authorities, and preparing the documentation and complying with the provisions can be quite involved, so it can be expensive to hire an attorney to set up such a partnership.

The limited partnership might be a good format to use in lieu of a joint venture, where each general partner is set up as a separate corporation or LLC. In this case, you use the limited partnership framework to bring in funds from the limited partners, who are sophisticated or knowledgeable investors or individuals with whom any of the general partners have pre-existing relationships.

C-Corporation

The C-corporation (C-corp) is the standard type of corporation, which is more commonly used if you are seeking funding for a company that will be producing an ongoing series of films, rather than for a particular project.

The advantages of setting up a corporation are the following:

- It's considered a separate entity, apart from the individuals in it, and it has liability for any debts or legal penalties. If you're creating a company designed to have a long-term existence, rather than simply producing a single film or slate of films, you have no personal liability because the corporation is a legal entity, so shareholders normally only risk the money they have invested, unless the corporation fails to follow the usual rules for running a corporation.

- It can be a good vehicle for raising anything from seed capital for a start-up to second- and third-stage financing as the company expands.

- It's easier to transfer corporate shares if anyone wants to buy them than to transfer an interest in a partnership or LLC.

- There are assorted tax benefits for the corporation, such as deducting the cost of employee benefits such as pensions, health insurance, and profit-sharing plans.

- If the corporation makes a profit, these earnings are paid to shareholders as dividends in proportion to each shareholder's ownership interests—although the managers may choose to limit dividends in order to invest a percentage of the profits into further development, such as producing more films, and those profits can then increase the value of each share of stock.

There are a few important disadvantages of the C-corp:

- There's a double-dipping tax, whereby the IRS taxes the corporation on its pre-dividend profits and also taxes shareholders on the dividends they receive. Then, too, if the film loses money, the corporation lists this as a capital loss, whereas most investors would prefer to use a loss to offset their income.

- There are assorted costs and special rules for managing a corporation, such as an annual franchise tax, regular shareholder and board of director meetings, records to keep, and reports to provide to shareholders.

- The investors will be particularly interested in the management team's track record, so if you're relatively new to putting together film projects and seeking funds, it's usually better to start with a partnership, joint venture, or LLC.

- The costs of offering shares may seem daunting, but you can seek a small amount of start-up capital to begin operations. Or, in lieu of cash for your shares, you might contribute the rights to a screenplay or other services you might provide, such as the payment you might expect for creating a short trailer, writing promotional copy, or setting up a marketing campaign, whereas other founding members contribute cash for their shares.

S-Corporation

One popular type of corporate structure is the S-corp, which is set up by meeting certain requirements of subchapter S of IRC Section 1362, which is where it gets its name.

The advantages of an S-corp include the following:

- All income, losses, deductions, and credits are passed on to shareholders on a per-share basis for taxation purposes, much as how a limited partnership or LLC is taxed.
- The S-corp is essentially a pass-through or flow-through vehicle, meaning that there's no double taxation on the entity, as occurs in a regular corporation. Should there be earnings and profits, these are taxed as dividends when they are distributed, but if there are no earnings and profits, there are no taxes.
- If the company expects to earn profits quickly and doesn't plan to reinvest earnings in the corporation (e.g., the S-corp is set up primarily for a single picture), then shareholders can quickly receive payments.

The disadvantages of an S-corp include the following:

- There have to be fewer than 75 shareholders, who must be individuals, an estate, or a qualified trust; they cannot be corporations or partnerships, and no foreign or nonresident alien shareholders are permitted.
- The corporation can only issue one class of stock; while the company can acquire corporate debt, it cannot be turned into a second type of stock.

Creating a Budget and Schedule

After you determine your structure for receiving funds, your next step is generally figuring out how much money you need, although sometimes you may first develop your budget to help you decide what kind of structure best suits your purpose for raising those funds.

You can include the budget in the business plan not only to indicate how much money you need for production, marketing, and promotion, but also so you can write a comparables section showing how well other films with a similar budget have done in the marketplace. You can additionally use the budget to project the likely return on investment (ROI) for investors, as well as to create rewards and perks for contributors in a crowdfunding campaign.

The Costs of Creating a Schedule and Budget

Creating the budget starts with creating a schedule that indicates how many days are needed for the film shoot based on the number of scenes and setups in the shoot and the particular cast and crew members needed each day for different locations. While you can use software, such as Movie Magic Scheduling and Movie Magic Budgeting from Entertainment Partners, to create the schedule and the budget, preparing a schedule and budget is a detailed and technical process, so it may be more economical in the long run to

hire someone who's experienced in preparing schedules
and budgets.

Preparing the Schedule

In order to prepare the schedule, follow these steps:

1. Conform the script so that the location for all of the
   scenes that occur in that location is described in the
   same way.

2. Break down and reorganize the scenes so that all of
   the scenes in one location are combined for shooting purposes, and these scenes are also grouped by
   actors, so that all the scenes in a particular location
   with the same actors—or most of the same actors—
   will be shot together (there may be modifications
   based on actor availability).

3. Figure out approximately how long a scene is expected to last and what actors or props are needed
   for that scene in order to create a day-by-day timeline for what scenes will be shot when. Factor in the
   time for setting up and taking down the needed
   equipment and moving from one place to another.
   A common rule of thumb is shooting 5 pages of
   script per day.

Commonly, the shooting schedule is used to calculate the budget, but sometimes, a filmmaker may start with a budget, and then the scheduler may have to adapt the schedule and the other elements in the budget to fit that target. Or later, on set, the director may make adjustments, such as adding new scenes or locations or consolidating shots in different locations into one, that increase or decrease the budget. Sometimes an unexpected increase in the budget may mean you need to secure additional funds—or you may have to do more cutting to reduce the budget so you can afford to make the film.

The unpredictable nature of filmmaking can lead to delays and increased costs, so normally, in writing the budget, an additional 10% is added to allow for such contingencies. If you need more than that, you'll need to go back to your initial investors or make an additional offering, or you'll need to alter the script to bring in the film on budget. In general, though, figure on creating a schedule and budget to determine what funds you need, and plan on working within the amount of funds you get.

An example of a shooting schedule can be found in the Appendix.

Preparing the Budget

Once the schedule is prepared, the budget can be created based on the cost of the actors, extras, vehicles, equipment, crew, locations, and other items required for each day on the set. Use a spreadsheet to keep track of all these items and make the calculations, so if anything changes, the budget can be easily changed. Having a budget can be used both to find funds and to adapt the script and plans for a less-costly shoot.

Budget Divisions

While there are some differences in the different categories and the items in different categories in preparing a budget, generally a budget is divided into "above-the-line" and "below-the-line" costs.

The above-the-line expenses include the cost of the script or story and the payment to producers, the directors, and the actors, including the travel and living costs paid to them.

The below-the-line category includes everything else, though this is often subdivided into other categories. For the production, the below-the-line category includes the other crew members, including those on the production staff handling set design, set operations, set dressing, property or props, wardrobe, makeup and hair, lighting, camera, production sound, transportation, locations, and craft services. It will also include any fringe benefits or payroll taxes for them.

The post-production costs include preparation of the film for editing, the editing, the music, a post-production bond, and creating the main and end titles.

Other expenses might include publicity, research and setting up screenings, legal fees, insurance, miscellaneous expenses, and the cost of obtaining financing, such as commissions and interest.

In creating these budgets, even if you only put the top sheet in the business plan, don't simply guess at your costs based on someone else's budget or a general idea of what the overall costs might be. An accurate estimated budget realistically reflects how much money you need to make the film and lets you know if you need to rework the script to reduce the costs.

An example of a budget can be found in the Appendix.

Creating a Producer Package

While you need a business plan to present to investors, you can use a producer package to pitch your project to get funding through pre-sales or licensing organizations, as well as to get funding and/or distribution deals from established producers, film studios, and other industry professionals. You might also use this package to secure advance commitments for product placements. This package can work in conjunction with a business plan, or you can incorporate much of the information in it into the business plan. Often it can stand alone, when you don't need a business plan.

A producer package includes these key elements:

- a script
- evidence of a copyright
- photos, bios, and credits of the actors who are interested or attached to the film
- a synopsis of the screenplay
- credits and bios of the director, producer, and top team members who are committed to the project
- the projected cost of producing the film, budget top sheet, or the complete budget.

Other information may be included, depending on who the package is for:

- location information.
- any press clippings about the project or those involved in it.
- details on any distribution or pre-sale agreements already set up; and
- an attractive glossy cover.

Creating a Business Plan

A business plan is essential for pitching the film or company to prospective investors; it's a plan for what you expect to do when you get the money, although it's not an agreement between you and the investor (for that you additionally need a private placement memorandum, or PPM). It isn't used in a crowdfunding campaign, unless you are seeking funds from investors, too, such as in the new equity crowdfunding approach.

You might create a business plan for your company, if you're planning a series of films and are seeking investors to buy shares in your company. However, more generally, if you're starting off, it's best to create a business plan for each film, whether you already have a legal structure for that or whether you intend to create one (as in the case of an LLC) once you have a commitment for funds for the film.

Think of a business plan as a marketing piece with financials to show the investor what the film is about and why it will appeal to its target market, the cost to make the film, how much it's likely to earn, and the investor's return under various high, medium, and low scenarios.

Include information about the following key elements, which are called by varying names in different plans but typically appear in this order:

1. An executive summary, usually written last, which summarizes the highlights of the other sections and makes a compelling case for financing your film.

2. Your company, including your goals and the members of your team.

3. Your film or films, including a synopsis of each.

4. The industry, including a discussion of the state of the film industry, a distinction between studio and independent filmmaking, and industry trends and projections.

5. The markets, featuring a description of your target markets, your plans to reach them, and a comparative analysis of comparable low-budget films.

6. New media and other nontraditional markets.

7. Distribution, including a discussion of the system for distributing independent films and your strategy for finding a distributor, as well as any attachments if you have letters of intent from name actors or distributors eager to distribute your film.

8. Promotion and marketing.

9. Risk factors, including a detailed warning about the high-risk nature of the film business (you're legally required to include this warning in your plan).

10. A financing and financial plan, which includes a discussion of how you intend to fund your film, along with

a budget summary and explanation of your plan to distribute any proceeds.

Feel free to write it in any order, except leave the Executive Summary section for last, because you won't know how to summarize the sections of the plan that you haven't written yet. A good rule of thumb is to write whatever you get information on first, which is often the film synopsis and company. Then, many find it easy to add in the information and risk statement, which is basically legal boilerplate, followed by the industry overview and market analysis and marketing strategy, because this information is readily available from reports, papers, and articles easily found through an Internet search. Plus, there's information on the industry and market available for purchase or subscription.

You can use photographs and graphics to dress up your plan, because this is a marketing and pitch document to entice investors to participate in your project—not just a plan for what you hope to do if you get the funds.

The Executive Summary

Write the Executive Summary like a hook to get the investor to bite and want to know more about your investment opportunity. Here, you lay out an overview of what's in the rest of the plan, but write it in a way to suggest that this is an exciting film and a great opportunity for achieving success with your management team. Keep this section to a page.

Give each section in the plan its own summary. Don't worry about the repetition; it helps to drive home your message and invites the prospective investor to read more about that section. One common approach is dividing your Executive Summary into two sections: (1) the Strategic Opportunity, and (2) the Investment Opportunity and Financial Highlights.

- In the Strategic Opportunity section, you describe the company, the film or films, the industry, the markets, and distribution.
- In the Company section, mention any well-known attachments among your team, such as if a member has directed or produced a successful film (and include their bios in the full Company section). Be sure to have a written consent from anyone you mention; otherwise you can quickly lose your credibility, and investors are likely to bail if you exaggerate or lie.
- In the Film(s) section, only include a line or two that makes each film sound intriguing, while providing the essence of the story, like the short log line for a TV show or a slogan you might see on a movie poster.
- In the Industry section, begin with an overview of the current state and key trends in the industry to provide a

context for introducing where your own company and film (or films) fit.

- In the Markets section, briefly indicate the target markets for your film, based on age, sex, ethnicity, or interest in a particular genre. If you are planning to do any marketing yourself, mention this here. Include any methods you hope to use (such as regular blogs and postings and Twitter) and why you think they will help sell the film.

- In the Distribution section, indicate whether you already have any distributors attached with written agreements who expect to distribute the film once it's produced. Or if you plan to self-distribute the film, note this here, and briefly state why you are well qualified or likely to be successful in using this approach. Note any special knowledge or experience you've had in distributing films before.

The Investment Opportunity and Financial Highlights section provides an overview of the financial information in your plan.

- Indicate how much money you're seeking to produce and distribute your film, and briefly note what you expect your worldwide box office and sales through other channels will be.

- Indicate your projected profit. Leave the details for your Financing section; if these figures look good, investors will often look at your management team next to see if you seem to have the ability to pull off what you describe in your plan.
- Point out that these numbers are merely projections, forecasts, or estimates. Otherwise, you can get in trouble with government authorities or open yourself up to civil suits by investors if you don't live up to your promises. Here, you also might mention any major risks.
- Consider concluding this section by indicating your plans for distributing any profits. Experts are divided on whether to include this explanation here or just with your other financials, so it's your call.

The Company

After the Executive Summary and Financing sections, the description of your company and your management team is the most important part of the plan. Prospective investors want to know they have a leadership group they can count on to carry out the plan, so they're especially concerned about the background of the leading team members—most notably the producer, director, and director of photography. If the writer of the script has previously been produced, so much the better.

Even if you or your team members have little experience in making feature films or full-length documentaries, you can still highlight related experience to show how you can make this happen. For example, if you've produced successful events, such as a big trade show, or a series of 5- to 15-minute shorts, that might show your readiness to produce a feature. Likewise, if the director or DP has directed or filmed many shorter projects, such as short narratives and commercials, this experience can be convincing, especially if the director or cinematographer has a reel or online link showing excellent work. It's even better if this past work relates in subject matter, theme, or style to the approach planned for this feature.

Start the section by describing your company aside from the team. Note what legal entity you have created or expect to form once funding is committed, such as an LLC or S-corp. Indicate when and where the legal entity will be or was formed, and briefly describe the company's purpose or mission. Include a brief description of your proposed film, its target market, its budget, your timetable for completing it, the type of distribution you'll be seeking (e.g., theatrical distribution, movies for TV or cable, direct-to-DVD or Blu-ray, foreign sales, Internet streaming, mobile downloads), and how you plan to arrange that distribution. Indicate the areas in which your company will be involved (e.g., development, production, distribution, and promotion).

Finally, describe the key members of your production team in a paragraph or two, and include any additional bio information in the appendix. In this bio, highlight any experience in the film industry, and include any applicable business experience in other industries, such as being a director on a TV show, being a cinematographer for travel ads, or being a producer of large community events. In the event that no one in your company has made a film before, find someone who has, and bring that person on board, even if it's just to act in a supervisory capacity. Their listing on your team will give you more credibility with investors—and once you're funded, their input can help you in making the film.

The Film or Films

In this section, describe the single film or series of films your company plans to produce (it's fine to repeat information from the Company section). For each film:

- Include a short synopsis, plus any elements that add commercial value to the project, such as whether it's based on a story that's been in the news and you have the life rights from a key player to tell his story. As in any synopsis, start with a compelling log line, or include an opening line (such as a quote that might appear on a movie poster) before the log line. Then, include two or three short paragraphs to convey the key plot or storyline of the script (and don't leave out the ending).

- Mention any scenes that might be controversial, such as scenes of graphic violence, rape, or nudity, so you don't mislead the investor.

- Include the film's genre, budget, target audience, writer, and location (if this needs to be filmed in a certain place). Add a line or two to mention any special facts that make your target audience a particularly desirable one to reach now, but don't mention any restrictions in shooting the film (such as plans to shoot it at a certain time of year).

- If you haven't selected a particular script, describe the size and genre of the types of films you plan to produce, and indicate that you are seeking development money to create or purchase scripts and expect to begin production by a certain date.

- Mention any attachments that make your project more valuable, in which any agreements are in writing, such as:
  - an exclusive option for a certain period of time on a property such as a life story.
  - an option on the rights to a published book, particularly if it has high sales.
  - an attachment of a star actor, director, or producer, reflected by a letter of intent; and
  - any money already committed to the project, including money you paid for an option.

- Indicate the planned budget for the film (just the total here, because the details will be in the Financing section). If you have partial financing, mention that.

In short, even in the initial development stage—even without a script or attachments—you can still hope to raise funds if you can make a convincing case for the films you hope to do with the team you've put in place by starting with a low budget and working your way up to higher-budget films as you get more experience.

The Industry

Although some potential investors may already be familiar with the film industry or part of it, write up the Industry section as if you are writing for an investor who knows little or nothing about the industry. Someone who already knows this information can easily skip it. Even if you are talking to industry insiders, this section is important to show that you are knowledgeable about the industry, which will help to reassure investors that you know what you are doing.

The key areas to discuss in this section include the following:

- How a film is made and gets to the theaters (keeping in mind that new investors may have unrealistic expectations).

- The major players in the industry (the six majors companies—20th Century Fox, Warner Brothers, Paramount,
  Columbia, Universal, and the Walt Disney Studios—
  and the mini-majors, which are the smaller production
  companies distributed by the majors); how the industry
  works; and a brief description of the box office arrangement to show why there are more opportunities for revenues, especially for an independent film, outside of the
  studio system.
- The distinction between studio and independent films
  (how each makes money, and the advantages and disadvantages of each).
- The size and scope of the industry (the size of the box
  office and other sources of marketing films, and the relative position in the box office of different types of films
  being produced).
- Your industry segment (the box office earnings and budgets for low-budget films compared to high-budget films
  in your industry segment).
- Future trends in the industry (likely developments in the
  industry over the next 3 to 5 years, including new venues
  and formats, as well as the potential impact of economic
  and political conditions).
- The role of your own company or film in the industry
  (where your own company and film or films fit, and how

you'll take advantage of the industry's overall trend of growth).

Be aware that the information about the industry is constantly changing, so include the latest data. If you are using material that was written more than a year or two ago, look for later information and update anything you have already written.

The Markets and Marketing Strategy

Look specifically at the market segments for your type of film and suggest how it might do in the box office and in other types of sales, based on what other films of the same type appealing to the same audience have done. Also, look at the budgets of these films to see how your budget compares, as a way to show that your proposed budget is a reasonable one. If you don't find a precise match, such as if your film combines two genres (e.g., a horror romantic comedy), then look at films from both genres. Draw on Box Office Mojo, Nash Information Systems, the MPAA, and other industry sources for this information, and turn the results into comparative tables.

Defining Your Market Segment

Your market segment is that segment of the whole film-going audience that is more likely to be interested in your type of film, which will affect your advertising and promotion campaign to pitch the film to this audience. You can break down your audience for films in several ways, according to the following categories:

- popular film genres, such as drama, comedy, action, thriller, horror, romance, sci-fi, and fantasy.
- theme, such as a political exposé or inspirational film.
- affinity group, such as an ethnic, racial, or religious group, or sports fans.
- age.
- sex; and
- similar budget

Describing Trends and Making Comparisons for Your Genre

After you do a breakdown by type of film, describe the recent trends for that genre and for the audience most interested in that type of film.

You might also discuss how the popularity of different genres goes in cycles, and if your film is designed to catch a currently popular wave, note this; if films of this type are currently out of favor, discuss how it's time for a revival, and provide examples of the times when this particular genre has done well. Should there be some commonality in the pattern you observe, such as if romantic comedies have done well during a time of economic upheaval and you're planning a romantic comedy for today's tumultuous times, point that out.

Another comparison is between your proposed budget and that of other low-budget indie films in your genre, especially films that have done well. Should your budget be significantly higher, point out the elements of your film that'll make it more successful and profitable, such as having a better director. If your moderate-budget film has mainstream crossover potential, compare it to films with similar budgets and point out what about your film will have broad appeal. There are several ways to obtain and organize this information:

- Get a list of the top domestic films, independent or not, that were released on 1,000 or fewer screens, with a budget under $5 million (or under your own). You can get this list from Variety or online through Baseline Studio System.
- Look at the year-to-year box office totals of the specialty films against which your film directly competes (normally reaching 1,000 screens or fewer, although a few breakouts such as *Juno* and *Little Miss Sunshine* have surpassed this limit).
- Compare the Oscar nominations of independent and non-independent films.

- Point out the few films that did especially well, especially if you encounter a downturn in the market generally for your type of film.

If you are doing a documentary, use the same basic approach, unless you are targeting the TV/cable market or educational market for your film.

Other Markets

Finally, discuss the other markets where you plan to release your film, the size and scope of these markets, and the total revenue you are likely to bring in annually in each one. Even if such returns are low now, most of these markets will experience substantial growth in the future; so an advantage of entering your film into these markets is that it can result in large future returns, as well as opening the door for you to more easily place new films in these revenue streams and providing you with a greater presence, so you get more sales in the future.

These other markets now include the following:

- TV and cable specials (a growing number of movies are made for TV, and well-known film actors are appearing in made-for-TV productions).
- mobile devices, including smart phones and tablets (on which viewers can easily download or stream videos).

- direct-to-DVD and Blu-ray (especially for genre films, although this market may be absorbed by the growing release of independent features on the Internet and mobile devices).
- streaming from commercial distributors such as Netflix (which offers downloading and streaming on home TV sets, computers, and mobile devices); and
- downloads and streaming from websites (including paid services).

Distribution

In this section, describe how the distribution process works (which many investors many not know), and more specifically, how you'll distribute your film through these various channels. Point out that filmmakers often have to advance the funds for distribution or expect the distributor to deduct expenses from the income received in addition to its distribution fee. Some of the points to make in this section include the following:

- Distribution deals can vary widely, from one in which the distributor pays for the distribution rights and becomes a partner with you in sharing proceeds to one in which the distributor expects the filmmaker to advance the prints and advertising (P&A) expenses, takes a distribution fee, and deducts its own expenses.

- The producer can turn over all film rights or can license specific rights to the distributor.

- Even though there's limited profitability, if any, in a domestic theatrical release, a theatrical release is still important because of the promotional value in selling in other markets.

- If it's possible to get picked up by a studio or mini-major, this is a big advantage because these companies have their own distribution divisions, so you'll have the advantage of their clout in the marketplace. The disadvantage is the high distribution fee the studio takes, commonly around 65% or more, although that can be offset by the much greater audience you get.

- Typically, an independent film will start off with a limited release in a few theaters. Then, as the film gains traction in the marketplace through favorable reviews and good word of mouth, it will expand to a growing number of theaters, as was the case for *Little Miss Sunshine*, which started off in about a dozen theaters and eventually was shown in about 1,500 theaters at its peak.

- It's also possible to get picked up for distribution by one of the studios or mini-majors, as described in the film industry overview.

- Distributors look for certain major elements (e.g., story, genre, attached cast, major players' past successes, tie-in with a known entity from another field, specialized audience, attached funds for marketing and promotion) in selecting the films they distribute, so note how you'll be creating a presentation to emphasize the strengths of your film. Have a trailer or screener to use in marketing the film, and point out how you can overcome any missing elements, such as not having any name actors, by having a film in a genre where a well-known cast isn't important, such as in the horror genre or in a film with a unique storyline.

- Include your plans for participating in major festivals, such as Sundance, Cannes, and the L.A. International Film Festival, or local festivals, where you can arrange showings, even if your film is not one of the official selections (and invite distributors to attend).

- Also plan to go to key film sales events, such as the American Film Market, to show your film as part of the event or to arrange for a private showing at a nearby theater. You can also meet with prospective distributors and use the event as a kind of promotional send-off in the hopes of picking up a national distributor.

- Make arrangements for distribution with a traditional domestic or international distributor before you enter into contracts for other types of distribution, since the traditional or international distributor will often want those rights. Keep your options open as you negotiate these arrangements, and describe how you'll explore these options in your business plan.

- High advances have been paid to some independent films that have done exceptionally well despite low budgets. For example, *Little Miss Sunshine* sold in 2006 for $10.5 million at Sundance.

- Once you line up a distributor, the distributor will make most or all of the marketing decision, such as deciding how to best position the film in picking its genre, creating and placing ads in the media, determining how to sell to theatrical exhibitors and foreign buyers, designing posters, and fashioning a PR campaign. Many distributors will also want to have control over the title and final cut of a film, or they may even ask for certain changes before they take over the film to make the film even more salable.

- While pre-sales are one of the holy grails of successful distribution, you normally have to complete a deal with a distributor first, and commonly distributors want to see a finished film so there's less risk. Moreover, you're in a better negotiating position for a better deal with a completed film. Still, it's possible to negotiate a deal with a partially completed film, where the distributor can at least see the film's quality and know when production will be completed, thereby gaining confidence in the finished product.

- There are different methods for releasing films based on anticipated audience size and available funds for marketing and promotion (i.e., big-budget films are released quickly by studios and distributors, and independent films are usually released moderately and slowly). This way, investors are prepared for a slower roll-out. Self-distribution may be an interim approach until you gain buzz for the film, which will enable you to get a distributor or deal with a larger independent producer. In this case, you might target specialty theaters in major cities and keep down the costs by setting up screenings at a time when the theater is usually not busy. With some local publicity, such as write-ups in the local newspaper and notices on Facebook and Twitter, you might get a large enough audience to pay for more showings. Then, you can continue expanding on your own this way or opt to turn everything over to a distributor or other independent producer.

- Despite the financing the investors are providing for production, and even for promotion and marketing, they can't control the distributor, and depending on the distribution deal, you may or may not receive any immediate revenue for the film. By providing this advisory, your investors don't have unrealistic expectations of what is possible.

Promotion and Marketing Plans

Traditionally, the distributor handles the marketing and promotion, but any promotion and marketing you do yourself can make a big difference in the attention paid to your film, so include a separate section to highlight and provide samples of anything you plan to do (e.g., a website for the film; a social media campaign; a sizzle reel, trailer, or short; press releases, blogs, posters, postcards, or other materials).

If product placement will be a key component in raising funds as well as creating promotional tie-ins, discuss this, too, especially if you have gotten some commitments. Mention the categories of products you expect to contact, such as car manufacturers or sporting organizations, but don't imply endorsements you might get if you haven't already gotten them, much as you shouldn't list A-list actors you would like to approach if you don't have letters of intent.

Risk Factors

Legally, you have to advise the investors of their risks, so provide a statement of anything that could go wrong to adequately warn potential investors of the different ways they could lose their money. Having a risk statement is also a good protection, because investors cannot later claim that they did not know the investment might not have favorable results.

Some of the risks to mention include the following:

- cost overruns because a film goes over budget;
- failure to meet production deadlines because it takes longer to produce the film than expected, due to delays during the film shoot or edit;
- problems with labor, suppliers, or distributors, such as a key actor becoming ill during filming or a distributor having problems with delivering films to theaters;
- sales projections not met because fewer viewers are seeing the film at theaters or downloading it on the Internet;
- unforeseen industry trends, such as a glut of films suddenly appearing on the same subject or a drop-off of interest in this topic, due to the cyclical nature of the film industry;
- competition, such as a new company making low-budget films in the same niche;
- unforeseen economic, social, or political developments, such as new recessions;
- technological developments, such as a new popular platform for downloading films, requiring a shift to a new format;
- inadequate capital because of cash flow problems due to unpaid debts;
- business cycles, such as a drop in business generally due to a slow-down in the economy; and
- other risks, including anything else you can think of that might affect the film business and the successful launch of your film.

Financing

This is where you explain how you plan to obtain your funding and what the investor will receive in return for an investment. Generally, this is a fairly brief section, since you don't want to provide an overview of how film financing works, in contrast to your explanation about film production and marketing, unless you'll be getting your funds from a number of different sources, such as pre-sales (indicate how much you have gained), gap financing (mention loans), and co-productions (explain what the co-producers are contributing to the film, such as cash or services).

Then, describe how any revenue will be paid to investors. Should you have a PPM, this will explain your offering in full detail, along with the legal language needed to comply with applicable security laws. Also, point out that the investor will not be affected by any profit participation of members of your production team, such as the lead actors, director, cinematographer, and editor, since that will come out of the producer's share of the profits (unless a famous actor or director has a percentage of the gross included in his or her contract).

Additionally, indicate when you expect to receive accounting statements—typically on a quarterly basis—from the different parties paying you these funds, such as distributors, foreign sales agents, producers reps, TV or cable networks, and purchasers of DVD/Blu-ray, Internet download, or streaming rights. Note that any indicated revenues will be paid within 30 days of receiving these statements.

Finally, note what to expect about residuals, which are normally paid (by the distributor, foreign agent, TV/cable network, or other responsible party) when your film is shown, to any talent in the union, should you have SAG or AFTRA actors in your film. If the party that is supposed to pay doesn't do so, you may become responsible, and in this case, the investors' interest will be second in line to those owed the residuals.

Types of Investors

There are all types of investors, and you should write your business plan to target the type of investor you're approaching; if you're submitting your plan to different types of groups, modify your plan accordingly, so you may have different versions of your plan. Each kind of funding source will have different requirements or conditions before they provide funds, and you can decide if you can accept those conditions. In other cases, a prospective investor may have certain demands, and you must decide if you are willing to meet those demands; otherwise, try to talk the prospective investor out of his or her request, work out a compromise, or make some of the requested changes but not those that would undermine the film's main message. Should you find the investor's demands are unreasonable, don't go after those funds.

Another caution is dealing with intermediaries who want money up front. Don't pay them anything. You should only pay a finder's fee from the funds you receive after the funds are in your bank and are fully cleared (be prepared to wait several weeks if these funds aren't put in through a wire, money order, or other recognized system for transferring funds). Let any prospective investor or intermediary know up front that you'll need this extra time for any checks to clear before you can pay a finder's fee.

Some major categories of investors, for whom you might slightly modify your business plan to build in the incentives to appeal to them, are the following:

1. Your family members, relatives, and friends may care less about the specifics of your business plan, and more about helping you out (and making some money, too), so there's no need to adapt your business plan to them.

2. Members of a church group or non-profit may be interested in investing in a film that supports and furthers their mission, so mention how your film will contribute to that purpose in your business plan, and when you do the comparative analysis in the financial plan, try to find examples of other films in your budget range that similarly support their mission.

3. Entrepreneurs and other business owners are individuals who have made money in something else (e.g.,
   communications, real estate, Internet, sports, finance)
   and are intrigued by the chance of having a fling with
   films. Some of their motivations include backing films
   with a message, participating in a new technology, or
   just thinking it would be fun. They also have a lot of
   money they can easily invest, although they like the
   idea of winning and want to back a project that will be
   successful. Thus, if you are going after these investors,
   you might highlight the opportunity for credits, coming to the set, having a small part in a crowd scene,
   meeting with the actors, or being an honored guest
   at a film launch party. The same appeals might work
   for business people who haven't joined the billionaire
   stratosphere but have become comfortably wealthy,
   such as successful doctors and dentists.

4. Special interest groups include nonprofit organizations, religious groups, foundations, and for-profit
   groups organized around a particular cause, and they
   may be interested in films that advance their agenda.
   Whatever the issue, if your film fits the profile, you
   might get funds from a group supporting that issue,
   and you should highlight that appeal in your business plan.

5. Previous and current clients with whom you have had
    a good relationship may be potential investors. If they
    like the work you have done for them on something
    else—particularly essential skills for filmmaking, such
    as writing, marketing, advertising, sales, organizing
    events, and cinematography—they may trust you, so
    they will put up some of the funding. If you feel that
    these clients have a substantial income and are realistic
    prospects, include them in your business plan, too.

6. Foreign investors have become a growing source of
    financing for independent films, as the market has
    become globalized and an increasing number of co-
    productions with foreign producers or films are shot in
    locations outside of the United States. While much of
    this foreign funding is going to established producers
    and production companies, there are still opportuni-
    ties, and a good place for making contacts is at events
    such as the American Film Market, which attracts dis-
    tributors, sales agents, and company principals from
    all over the world. Should your film involve characters
    from a particular country or a topic of special interest
    to a country, such as a lead who comes from Greece
    or has opened up a popular Greek restaurant, then
    that would set the stage for approaching investors
    from that country.

7. Location-specific or event-specific investors may fit
   into your plan, especially if your film takes place in a
   location where you might find funds. For instance, if
   you'll be shooting the film in a city or small town that
   is prominently featured as a character in the film—not
   just a location that could look like anywhere—then
   a fundraising campaign based on appealing to local
   pride might be the ideal way to get funds. Should you
   be organizing special events to raise funds, or if your
   film lends itself to events with specialty parties (e.g.,
   the motorcycle community), you can mention this,
   too. And if your film is a natural for certain types of
   product placements (e.g., getting funds from companies making motorcycles), mention your plans to seek
   such placements, but don't mention any brand names
   until you get commitments.

What to Offer Investors

In seeking out investors, the usual approach is to offer
50% to those investing in the film, with a split between the
investors who provide the total budget and with the commission from any intermediary finding the funds taken
off the top. Should there be more than one investor, you
split up the 50% shares to the investors based on their
proportional contribution to that 50%. Normally, any
percentages, commonly expressed as "points," to team

members come out of the producer's share unless you have an agreement to the contrary with investors, such as specifying that these will come out of the first revenues received for the film, and thereafter the investors will receive their percentage followed by the regular investor/producer split. For example, if an investor puts up the funds for 20 shares in an offering of 100 shares, he would have a 20% ownership of the investors' percentage or 10% of the whole company. However, while the investors might be in line to get a 50% share of the proceeds or shares in the company, many filmmakers offer a slightly higher return on their investment of 110% to 120% before splitting up the net profits.

Another perk that many filmmakers offer investors is a credit in the film. Typically, a single investor providing all of the funding or a few investors providing a substantial contribution each will receive an executive producer credit, with the differing contributions sometimes recognized in the roll of credits by featuring the biggest investor in an executive producer credit by himself, and then listing the investors contributing a smaller amount together under another executive producer credit. However, reserve these executive producer credits for substantial funders only. Those contributing less might be recognized as "supporters" or "contributors" in the acknowledgments and thank-yous that scroll by on the screen.

Obtaining Film Incentives

If you expect any incentives in the form of state, county, or city discounts (e.g., rebates, tax credits for the film company, and transferable tax credits for local individuals and companies), include those here and in your budget. Arranging for these incentives will contribute to your credibility by showing that you know how to get the best deal for your film, as well as reducing the money needed from investors.

Many states have passed legislation to be competitive in attracting the film industry to the state, and many counties and cities have their own programs. Because these incentives vary greatly and change from year to year, check on the websites of the states, countries, and cities where you want to film to see what incentives, if any, they offer, or check the website of the Association of Film Commissioners International to find out which states, counties, and cities offer incentives.

In deciding whether to include a particular incentive in your business plan, consider any limitation that may affect whether that incentive will work for you. For example, most states first determine how much you have spent at the end of your production before they pay the agreed-upon incentive, which means you'll still need your whole budget in place before you start filming. However, you can still use this possible incentive to show the return you'll get after you complete production, such as promoting the film and entering it in festivals with the incentive money you receive.

Also, take into consideration any costs of bringing your cast and crew to the location offering the incentive to determine if the savings from the incentive are enough to offset any extra costs of transporting your cast and crew.

Financial Plan

Your financial plan is where you crunch all the numbers together to show the prospective investor what the film is likely to net after all the costs are deducted, thereby providing a return on investment (ROI) based on low, medium, and high projections. A lot of these projections may be wishful thinking, even in the low return scenario. But as best you can, show how the data you have assembled demonstrates that other films that compare in terms of theme and budget have done as well, by incorporating the relative influence of your genre, stars, director, distribution, and ancillary returns.

If you are not mathematically inclined, bring in someone who is good with details and numbers to do this part of the proposal, whether a part of your company or an outside hire. If you do it yourself, there are software programs that will help you create this plan, or you can start with the financial plan of a company with a comparable film and change the numbers to correspond to your own film project.

However you do it, your financial plan should include examples of a few previously released comparable films, where you show their profits and use that as a basis for estimating the likely profits of your film based on your estimated revenues and costs. If you have previously featured these films in your marketing section to illustrate the potential box office return, summarize that data here to highlight the financials for each film. A sample list of comparable films from the past 10 years, with corresponding budgets and percentage returns, can be found in the Appendix.

Sources of Data

Information on comparable films is available from various sources, many of them free:

- Box Office Mojo (http://www.boxofficemojo.com)
- Nash Information Services (http://nashinfoservices.com/)
- IMDb, which offers free information (http://www.imdb.com/chart) and detailed box office information for a monthly subscription fee (http://pro.imdb.com/boxoffice/alltime-us). You can then pull out the information on the all-time gross and the budget for films comparable to yours.
- The Numbers (http://www.the-numbers.com)
- *Variety*, which has a section for "Charts" (http://www.variety.com/charts) and a section where you'll find the weekly box office for films in domestic release, which includes

the cumulative amount for as long as the film has been in release. *Variety* includes some films released by the independent divisions of the majors and mini-majors, as well as an indie films release chart for independents that have been picked up by larger distributors, such as Lionsgate.

- *The Hollywood Reporter*, which requires you to be a subscriber to get the box office charts (http://www.hollywood-reporter.com/business/charts). These box office figures include Canada as well as Puerto Rico, so they might be more accurately described as domestic or North American box office results, although the vast majority of results come from the United States.

- Baseline (http://www.baselineresearch.com) has even more detailed up-to-date data on more than 140,000 released films and TV programs, and 13,000 film and TV projects in development. You may even qualify for a free trial by going to their Studio System website (http://www.studiosystem.com).

The advantage of having multiple sources for your data is that you can double-check the results, as well as find information on films that are listed on one source but not another.

Describing Your Assumptions

In order to provide a rationale for how you have gotten your numbers, include your assumptions in your business plan before you present your tables. You may not need to include your assumptions if you're only presenting your plan to people in the industry who already know this information. Alternately, if you include your assumptions, industry pros can skip over them, or have two versions of your plan—the complete one, which you present to those outside the industry, and the slimmed-down plan for those in the know.

The key assumptions for your summary projected income table are the following:

- Domestic theatrical rentals: this is the percentage of the theatrical box office that is returned to the distributor or producer based on the split with the exhibitor.
- Domestic ancillary or other revenue: this is the revenue received from all nontheatrical sources, which includes cable, DVD/Blu-ray, video, network and syndicated television, pay-per-view, Internet, and streaming video.
- Foreign theatrical and ancillary revenue: this in all revenue received by the distributor for all box offices and other sources outside of the United States, Canada, and Puerto Rico.
- Production and other costs: this includes both the above-the-line costs for the producers, actors, and directors, and the below-the line costs for the crew and other expenses, as described in the budget. These costs also include the releasing costs, distribution expenses, or prints and

advertising (P&A) costs for releasing and advertising the film. Besides the costs for the initial release, there will be continuing costs as the film remains in distribution.

- Gross income: this is the projected pre-tax profit after deducting the direct expenses for distribution, including the production and P&A costs, before deducting the distributor's fees and overhead expenses.

- Distributor's fees: this is the percentage of the revenues paid to the distributor, which is commonly 35% of the distributor domestic and foreign gross revenues, and excludes the distributor's out-of-pocket expenses.

- Net producer/investor income: this is the project's pre-tax profits to be split between the producers and investors, based on the agreed-upon split of shares held by investors.

- Summary projected cash flow: this is the moderate-profit expected cash flow based on a comparison with other films chosen (based on their budget, genre, theme, and approach), although their profitability does not guarantee that this film will be successful.

- Alternate revenue scenarios: these three scenarios show low (or break-even), moderate, and high projections, based on the data from the tables showing the profits of selected comparable films. In the low revenue scenario, the film breaks even, so some or all of the production costs are covered, but there's no profit. The moderate

revenue scenario, which is considered the most likely result for the film, is used for a cash flow projection. Finally,
the high revenue scenario is based on the film doing as
well as the very successful films in your category, although
investors should consider this a best-case scenario, since
it's unpredictable whether this film will do as well.

Creating Your Financial Plan Tables

Various formats are used for these tables, but basically you
want to create 3 or 4 different tables that show the following:

- A comparable films table features at least 5 comparable
  films that show a positive profit, indicating the net inves-
  tor/producer profit (figuring on a 50-50 split) in which
  the cost to create the film is deducted from the total producer's gross. In this chart, you show the results for each
  picture and the average investor/producer profit. Then,
  you show what the results would be if you deduct your
  own film's costs. Different producers organize this table
  in different ways. One approach is to create a summary
  table where you list the gross and cost of each film to
  determine the net profits. A sample table can be found
  in the Appendix.

- An income projections table predicts how much your
  film might make under medium, low, and great success
  scenarios. Start with your average domestic box office

and home video from your comparable films table, but then add in other categories and numbers, including deducting the exhibitor's share and adding in your pay TV numbers, your foreign and gross based on the latest rates, and your gross ancillary revenues (a good source of this data is Baseline Studio System). After you combine all of this information on separate tables to get an average for the comparable films, you plug these into your summary table. Then, you deduct your distributor costs and the production or negative costs to arrive at the net investor/producer profits. Finally, obtain your success projections. To get the low success projections, increase your budget by 20%; to get the high success projections, subtract your low success box office gross from your medium success gross (i.e., the average of your comparable domestic box office and home video numbers—if you feel the average is too high, reduce it by 50%, 25%, or some other number), and then add the results to your medium box office gross to create your high box office gross.

- A projected cash flow analysis may not be necessary if you are seeking funding for a single film, but if you are raising funds for several films or for a company to produce films, do a cash flow analysis based on a moderate profit scenario. In this analysis, use the more likely return on your film, and show by quarter when you'll spend your budget money, when you expect to receive different revenues, and when you have to pay for various fees and P&A expenses. There's no need to use the period when you are looking for money, since you haven't really started on production, even though you may be working on the script; if you have 1 film, use a 3-year cash flow breakdown; for 2 or more films or a company, break it down for 5 years. A sample projected cash flow table can be found in the Appendix.

- Another way to do it, for an even more precise breakdown for each film, is to show your income and costs in various categories, such as gross film rentals, home video rentals, pay TV revenues, distributions fees, and P&A, to indicate your total and cumulative cash at that point and the return to investors.

- A projected investor returns table summarizes everything to show the total cash returned to the investor/producer, less the production costs, and the investor's priority return, which is the amount of money you give back to the investors before splitting any profits—and all of these under the low, medium, and high returns scenarios. Essentially, you take the total cash returned to investors from your totals in the cash flow table, deduct the production costs, take out the investor's priority return (the money the investor already put in), calculate the adjusted investor/producer profit, figure out the investor's 50% share, and determine the total cash returned to the investor over the 3-year period of release—plus, there still could be more from later residuals. You can also use this data to calculate the investor's ROI by taking the net investor return and dividing it by the amount invested by the investors.

The table you present in your report might represent summary tables, in which you have combined the results from a worksheet. If so, put the worksheets in an appendix or let prospective investors know they are available if they want to know how you arrived at your data.

Packaging and Presenting Your Business Plan

Once you have all the sections completed for your business plan, think about how to package and present it so it stands out and looks good. For example, you might include photos from a film shoot to create your trailer in the report; you might also include photos of the members of your team. Some filmmakers package their plan in a binder with sleeves on either side, so they can present the business plan on one side, and any supporting PR materials, such as press releases, testimonials, and news clips, on the other. Others use a loose-leaf binder. Some package it in a glossy cover. However you do it, make sure your presentation looks very professional so it makes a good impression on the investor.

Creating a Private Placement Memorandum (PPM)

The business plan is like a marketing or sales document to present your film, series of films, or company to investors. Once investors indicate an interest in investing, you additionally need an agreement about what funds you are receiving, what you'll do with those funds, and how the investors will receive a return on their investment if the film, films, or company make money. This agreement can take the form of a contract, although commonly, film producers use a private placement memorandum (PPM).

While you can find a PPM boilerplate or create your own PPM document online through a company such as Rocket-Lawyer (http://www.rocketlawyer.com), a fee-based service where you answer questions about your offering to create the document, you should have your offering written or reviewed by a lawyer who is experienced in creating such agreements. This legal input is critical because not only are you creating a legal document that will be binding on you and your investors, but you also have to be in strict compliance with SEC regulations. However, the more you can do yourself, the better, since attorneys typically charge $5,000 and up for preparing this document, and it will cost much less for just the legal review.

The PPM essentially indicates how many shares of stock you are offering at what price, the minimum number of shares an investor can buy, how much the company intends to raise, who is involved in the company, the risk involved in the offering, the need for the investor to be an accredited (i.e., wealthy) investor, and how many shares the company expects to keep for itself (typically half of the issued shares).

If you are meeting with an attorney to discuss a PPM or filling out an online interview to generate a PPM document, you'll need to answer these key questions:

- What is the name of your company?
- What is the maximum number of shares of common stock being offered by the company?
- What is the purchase price of each share?
- What is the maximum and minimum number of shares an individual investor can purchase?
- What is the minimum number of shares that must be purchased in order for this offering to take place? (In other words, what's the minimum you need to produce the film?)
- When does this offering terminate? (In other words, when is the final date for investors to purchase a share under this memorandum?)
- What is the date when this PPM will be mailed or presented to potential investors?
- When was the company established (i.e., registered)?
- Who is the founder of the company?
- How many people are currently working in the company?

- What is the initial capital investment for the company? (In other words, how much did you and any associates put up to found the company, including the fees to incorporate?)

- What is the capital investment contribution of the founder? (In other words, what percentage of this initial investment came from the founder?)

- In which year did the company introduce its first product to the market? (In other words, when did you create, purchase, or option the script you'll be filming?)

- When did the company reach the break-even point? (If you are just starting the company, this won't apply, so you might use your cash flow analysis to suggest when this break-even point might occur.)

- What is the projected profit for the current fiscal year? (You might use the year when you first started pre-production or production, when you first got your investment funding, or your projected profits based on extending your cash flow analysis for 3 years, since typically a film won't start to reap profits until its second year).

- Describe the intended use of sale proceeds (i.e., for production of your film). Should you have more than one intended use for the proceeds, indicate that, and break down the amount of the investment that is going to each use (e.g., to produce a film, and to market and promote it).

- What is the capitalization of the company prior to the offering? (This could be nothing, if you are just starting; otherwise, the total capitalization is the total bonds, debt obligations, and all types of equity that make up the company's capital structure.)
- Which state laws govern this offering (commonly the state where the business is registered)?
- How many shares have previously been issued by the company (including any shares held by shareholders, the owner, officers, directors, or other persons having an interest in the company)?
- List the number of shares currently owned by each shareholder who owns a minimum of 5% of the current shares in the company. Then, list the name of the shareholder who owns any shares and the number of shares owned.
- What is the total number of shares owned collectively by all officers, directors, and employees of the company?
- What is the company strategy? (In other words, what does the company plan to do for its growth and development? Provide investors with a positive image of the company's business plan.)
- What is the marketing strategy of the company? (In other words, how does the company plan to achieve continued growth through its marketing?)

- List the current directors, officers, or other individuals with substantial control over the business. (If it's just you right now, that's fine.)
- Who will provide information about the company and its offering if requested by a potential investor? (Include the name of that individual, which might be you, and a phone number.)
- Who is the potential investor? (List the name of a particular person you are contacting, or if you are approaching multiple investors, leave this answer blank.)

A sample PPM can be found in the Appendix.

CHAPTER 3

Creating a Crowdfunding Campaign

An alternative to getting funding from investors is the crowdfunding campaign, where you ask contributors to donate money to your campaign in return for rewards or perks. You cannot appeal to contributors as investors, since that would be a violation of SEC regulations, which require registration for anything beyond a private placement to a limited number of accredited investors. However, as of January 1, 2013, there's a new law that will permit equity crowdfunding to seek investors for offerings of less than $1 million.

The crowdfunding law was signed in the spring of 2012, called the JOBS Act, short for Jumpstart Our Business Start-ups. This makes it possible for the general public to participate in equity crowdfunding, where they can receive company equity in exchange for contributing funds, once the SEC issues its regulations. It is expected, according to a report from Crowdfunding Capital Advisors, a crowdfunding industry consulting firm, to be issued in September 2013, and the equity crowdfunding space is expected to generated at least $4.3 billion in investment. Under the law, individuals with annual incomes of less than $100,000 can invest up to 5% of their income, while those who make more than $100,000 can invest up to $100,000. While the SEC is formulating its regulations, crowdfunding platforms need to operate under the license of a broker-dealer.

However, while the law passed, it is still limited to accredited investors in the United States. Thus, an individual can market an equity online, but only to accredited investors, until the SEC works out the regulation issues for investors. In the meantime, you need to go through a broker who has a commission to act as a equity crowdfunding portal.

The main reason for the lag in implementing the law is that the SEC is moving slowly in implementing the law's two most important provisions—one allowing individuals to generally advertise private investment offerings and another allowing unaccredited investors to participate. Still, a few companies are already completing transactions, according to Humayun Khan, author of "Why the JOBS Act Hasn't Launched Equity Crowdfunding," in the hopes that the SEC will allow the pending provisions of the JOBS Act quickly enough to launch their offerings. Among these are EarlyShares, which partnered with Point Capital Markets, CircleCup, and FundersClub. Many of the platforms expect to conduct funding activities in partnership with broker-dealers who will actively manage the transactions and funds raised from the investors in return for a broker's fee of about 8½%. Another reason for the delay is to protect unsophisticated investors.

There are now several hundred platforms for raising funds in this way, although the major platforms for raising funds for films and other types of products and services are Kickstarter (http://www.kickstarter.com), Indiegogo (http://www.indiegogo.com), and RocketHub (http://www.rockethub.com). With all of these programs, you set a goal of how much you want to raise and a time limit in which to raise these funds (commonly 30 to 45 days). With Kickstarter, it's an all-or-nothing proposition: the funds are held in an escrow account, and either you get them after you meet your goal or they are returned to the contributors and you don't get anything. With Indiegogo, you get whatever you've raised at the end of your campaign. With some other programs, you get whatever money has been contributed every couple of weeks.

The Growth of Crowdfunding

Crowdfunding, also known as crowd financing, involves individuals collectively networking and pooling their resources, usually through the Internet, to help the efforts of other individuals or organizations. While it has been used to fund all sorts of activities, from the creative work of artists and musicians to community programs and software development, it has become an especially popular means of funding films. For example, out of the nearly 6,500 individuals and organizations who met their funding goals as of November 5, 2012, about 10% of these were for films, or about 650 films.

Until recently, crowdfunding strictly required those seeking funds this way to clearly indicate that any funds received were to be considered contributions in return for rewards or voluntary donations to support the cause and perhaps receive recognition as a result. But on April 5, 2012, President Obama signed into legislation the JOBS Act, which permits equity crowdfunding, in which a company can sell small amounts of equity to a large number of investors. The SEC has been charged with setting forth specific rules and guidelines specifying what kind of investments are possible.

One rule that has already been advanced is that crowdfunding offerings will count toward the higher limit of investors permitted without having to register the offering with the SEC, permitting companies to raise money from publicity and other media such as the Internet. Moreover, crowdfunding offerings will count toward the higher registration threshold that permits up to 2,000 or more accredited investors, or up to 500 unaccredited investors, without registering.

This new equity crowdfunding approach is quite different from the contribution model of crowdfunding used so far, in that a company seeking money through equity financing can sell up to $1 million in securities in any 12-month period to an unlimited number of investors, rather than seeking contributions that involve no company ownership. Moreover, companies using the crowdfunding exemption must make this offering through an intermediary that is registered as a broker (who can promote securities and solicit investors) or a "funding portal" (who cannot) with the SEC. And in contrast to making donations in traditional crowdfunding, these contributors will be investors getting shares in return for their funding.

Generally, the advantage of the crowdfunding approach is it that it reduces the risk of starting a company or seeking money for a film. It also helps to filter out the bad ideas, because they won't find investors—although another big reason for not reaching your goal could be that people don't know about your offering because you didn't sufficiently promote it.

The Rise of Crowdfunding

Crowdfunding got its start in the music industry back in 2000, when ArtistShare set up a crowdfunding website for music, which was followed by a few other sites, including SellaBand in 2006, Indiegogo in 2008, PledgeMusic in 2009, Kickstarter in 2009, RocketHub in 2010, InvestedIn in 2010, and GoFundMe in 2010.

The crowdfunding industry has been growing rapidly. It funded more than 1 million campaigns in 2012, up from 81% the previous year, with Western markets account for about 95% of the market.

According to Deloitte, a major financial auditing and advisory company, crowdfunding portals are espected to raise $3 billion in 2013, up from $1.5 billion in 2011. While there are many types of crowdfunding sites, including conxsumer lending, the largest category, reward-based portals such as Kickstarter and IndieGoGo, are the second largest category. This category is expected to raise over $700 million in 2013, while the donations market contributing to a good cause is expected to be worth over $500 million in 2013.

According to Ryan Caldbeck, a career private equity investor, writing in June 2013 in Forbes (Crowdfunding Trends: Which Crowdfunding Sites Will Survive," June 23, 2013), there are over 500 active crowdfunding platforms. Kickstarter, the leader, has raised $371 in its first 3 ½ years of existence, and now is up to $574 in funds raised.

What Makes Crowdfunding Work?

Although crowdfunding has become a proven vehicle for raising funds, not all campaigns are successful. In fact, Kickstarter's success rate is only 44%. So what works, and what doesn't? Here are some general principles:

- Have a good campaign video and effectively word your appeal.
- Provide incentives and offer rewards that appeal to donors across the spectrum (from high to low contributions). Make certain you can afford your promotional discounts, giveaways, or advance purchase discounts when it comes time to deliver.
- Stand out from the growing clutter of projects vying for attention with a powerful promotional campaign using both your personal network and the media to spread the word. Show your personality.
- Show people how their money can be used to mean something, including enabling you to be a creator you couldn't be otherwise.
- Show people that they are part of something that others support and feel is important. To help start the process, have a couple of friends show their support for you by contributing.
- Be a friend, whereby you give your fans something extra that you would only give your friends, such as some inside information or an invitation to a special event or exclusive party.
- Show continuity by continuing to do what you do to help givers feel that their money will be used for more great stuff.

- Research what others competing for contributors in your category are doing. Notice what those who are successful have done, and compare them to those who have not met their goal.
- Create several videos and plan to rotate them throughout your campaign. Each video should be less than 5 minutes long and should clearly indicate what you are offering and why this is something that's needed. You can use links to YouTube to embed your video.
- Be ready to interact with your fans when they ask questions or offer feedback either through the crowdfunding site or through social media or e-mail. Be open to their recommendations for perks, rewards, or incentives.
- Reach out to the media as another potential source of coverage.
- While you do need to reach out to your network to let them know your campaign is seeking contributions, don't overdo it.

Besides these general recommendations for using a crowdfunding platform, the major platforms offer guidelines for making their specific crowdfunding program work. Here are the recommendations from the big three: Kickstarter, Indiegogo, and RocketHub.

Kickstarter

Begin with a concrete, precisely defined project and come up with some desirable rewards. In deciding what to offer, the primary rewards should be things from the project itself; that is, backers should be given things that are cool that they helped make possible with their contributions.

The four common types of rewards that appear on Kickstarter are the following:

- Copies of the thing, such as a DVD or print from the show. Price these items at what they would cost if bought in a store.
- Creative collaborations in which the backer is involved in the project, such as becoming an extra in the film or having their voice recorded for the soundtrack. Price this and the following items based on what might be appropriate for your audience.
- Creative experiences, which the backer might not be able to get otherwise, such as visiting the set, getting a phone call from the director, having dinner with the cast, or having a scene shot at his or her house.
- Creative mementos, which might include JPEGs or prints from the location of the film shoot, thanks in the credits, or other meaningful tokens related to the project.

It's important to have both high- and low-priced rewards. In its own research, Kickstarter found that the most popular pledge amount was $25, and the average pledge was around $70. But projects with lower-priced perks were more likely to succeed.

Because Kickstarter has an all-or-nothing model, be realistic in what you set as your goal, and factor in the cost of producing and delivering the rewards to backers. While you can always raise more than your goal and keep that, you can't raise less. If necessary, you can always kick in the difference in the last few hours before the campaign ends if you are close to your goal but not quite there.

For your project deadline, you can set it for anywhere from 1 to 60 days, although Kickstarter has found that projects with the highest success rates last no more than 30 days. One reason for this is that it takes a lot of intensive, hard work to run a successful Kickstarter campaign, and shorter projects help show that you'll be able to put in this effort, so backers feel more confident that you can do it and are motivated to join you. Then, too, if you put on a shorter Kickstarter campaign first, and raise the funds and complete the project, it shows that you can complete a larger project; this prior success encourages backers to believe in you and want to support your next campaign. By contrast, longer-duration campaigns may seem less urgent to backers, and you may procrastinate in promoting the campaign, which usually leads to failure.

Having a good video is another key to success, as campaigns with videos have a 50% success rate versus 30% for those without one. Most of these videos are fairly simple, but if you are proposing a film, it's a good idea to include a short trailer, sizzle reel, or examples of the work of the principal cinematographer to suggest what the quality of the finished film will be like.

In this video, Kickstarter recommends that you do the following:

- Say who you are and put your own face in the video.
- Tell the story behind your project to indicate where you got the idea, what stage your project is currently in, and how you are feeling about it.
- Ask for people's support, and explain why you need the money and what you'll do with it.
- Talk about your rewards, and present them visually.
- Explain that you won't get anything if you don't reach your goal.
- Thank everyone for their contribution.
- Provide your own music or get some free or low-cost music from resources such as SoundCloud, Vimeo Music Store, Free Music Archive, and ccMixter.

Other recommendations for your Kickstarter project include the following:

- Have a specific, memorable campaign title. Avoid words such as "help," "support," or "fund," which suggest you are asking backers to do you a favor rather than providing them with a great experience they will love.
- Pick a strong project image that both accurately reflects your project and looks good.
- In your description, briefly and clearly tell prospective backers what your project is about and what you hope to accomplish. It should be something you might be able to convey in a single tweet.
- Include a bio where you describe more about you and why you are the best person to lead this project. If you have links to prior work, share those, since that plays a key role in gaining your backer's trust.

Once you post your project information online, promote it. Though you might get support from all over the Internet, start with support from your own network and their networks. You have to tell people about your project to get their backing, and you must do so more than once in a variety of ways. Some of the ways suggested by Kickstarter include the following:

- Effective outreach to your personal networks. A good start is to send a personal e-mail to your close family and friends, so they can get in on the ground floor. Then, use Facebook, Twitter, and your personal blog to spread the word to your followers.
- Create real-world events and connections. Talk about your campaign with others. You might put on pledge parties or organize meetups through a group like Meetup to let people know what you are doing. Print up posters or flyers to distribute to your community.
- Contact the media, such as your local newspaper, TV, or radio stations. Or pitch your project to blogs and online media that might be interested in your type of project, especially as you start to build a following.
- But avoid spamming. Some things not to do include posting your link on other Kickstarter project pages, repeatedly sending links on Facebook or @messages on Twitter, and generally over-posting anywhere.

Kickstarter also recommends using the project's update as a regular blog to let others know how you are doing, share any media coverage, and thank your backers. If you have pictures from an event related to your project, post those as well. You can choose whether the update should go only to your backers or to everyone; either way, it helps to build momentum for your project.

If your project is funded, let backers and others know what is happening and even ask them for feedback. Celebrate your successes with your backers, too, such as by sharing reviews, press coverage, and photos from your project as you execute it. For instance, you might send photos from the set as it's filmed. Additionally, make arrangements to fulfill the rewards you promised. You might even have a fulfillment party with friends to help you package and send out the rewards.

Indiegogo

The recommendations for pitching your film on Indiegogo are much the same as on Kickstarter, and they have a fixed funding platform where you can go for broke and have a slightly lower commission rate (4%)—although then you get nothing and pay nothing if you don't make your goal, just as with Kickstarter. Or you can choose what most people using Indiegogo do: flexible funding, with a lower commission if you make your goal or go over (4% plus a 3% credit processing fee), and higher if you get less than that, but at least you get to keep it (9% plus the 3% fee). If you have nonprofit status, you can arrange for Indiegogo to deduct 25% from your fees.

As with Kickstarter, you set a funding goal and deadline, which you can't change. However, you don't have to put all your eggs in one basket by having a single campaign for a large project; instead, you can divide it up into parts, which may be an especially good approach for filmmakers (e.g., running a separate campaign for your pre-production development stage, another for production in doing the film shoot, a third for post-production in getting your film edited, and a fourth for distribution, which would include marketing and promotion). Two award-winning films— *Sound It Out* and *You've Been Trumped*—used this approach.

Indiegogo also suggests setting your goal by estimating how many people you need to donate to meet your goal and assessing whether you can attain that many contributors.

Another key consideration is "goal psychology," which is the way people view and respond to your goal. If you set your goal too high, people may feel your goal is unattainable; if you set it too low, people may think you are being unrealistic. So choose a goal that appears reachable and reflects your real needs. In fact, Indiegogo recommends that you include a detailed budget in describing your pitch to indicate how you'll use the money.

As for setting your deadline, you have up to 120 days for a flexible funding campaign or up to 60 if you go for fixed funding. But it's best to set a deadline based on raising funds throughout your campaign, and you have to be able to actively manage the process (which can include providing regular updates, sending out announcements to your network, and regularly checking your progress). A deadline of 40 to 50 days is short enough to convey urgency but long enough to create momentum.

Take into consideration when you need the money, since you may have to wait up to 2 weeks to get it after the campaign ends. And plan on raising funds the first day of your campaign, which is when the countdown to your deadline begins. Should you need more time for planning your campaign, take the extra time before you launch so you really are ready.

As with Kickstarter, tell a compelling story about why people should find your campaign deserving of their money. You want to build their passion for your project and their trust in you, since that's what gains support. Don't just present your project, but introduce yourself and your background, too, and explain why your project is important to you.

Having a video along with your pitch text is critical, since campaigns with videos are more likely to be funded or raise more money on the average than projects without one. But both video and text are important and should supplement each other. Some people will read your text first and, if interested, will go to the video to learn more, while others will first look at the video, and if the video hooks them, they will look at the text.

A powerful pitch video includes these key elements:

- Who are you? Describe yourself, your team, and your story.
- What project are you raising money for? Be specific, including describing your budget.
- When and where will your project happen?
- How can people participate and assist you, aside from contributing money?

It also helps if you have a team working with you, since Indiegogo has found that campaigns with teams raise 80% more funds than projects run by an individual do. With a film project, teams are already a given, since you usually need at least 3 to 5 key people heading up your crew to create the film—so list those you are starting with, and as you add additional team members, you can always add them to your campaign.

A good way to develop a great pitch is to look back at previous "Success Stories" in your genre to view their presentations. This can also help you select your perks, which are very important to your success, since they give contributors a non-monetary item of value as an incentive to support your campaign. Such perks can be almost anything, including items mentioned in the Kickstarter section, but there are certain things you can't offer, such as anything that's illegal or a monetary return on the money contributed, share of a company, share of profits, or loan repayment (since this is a contribution, not an investment or loan).

On Indiegogo, you can offer up to a total of 12 perks; Indiegogo suggests starting with 3 to 7 perks, so you can easily add more perks after you launch—and sometimes you may get suggestions from fans about new perks to add. You can drop perks only if they haven't been claimed yet. The best perks are tangible and tailored to your contributors. You can get ideas from previous successful film campaigns, and some suggestions that are particularly appropriate to film projects include the following:

- discounts or coupons, such as to a party or fundraiser
- goods such as your DVDs, Blu-rays, film posters, and photos from the set (pre-sold)
- a party or private event for your contributors
- merchandise with your logo on it, such as T-shirts and postcards
- producer credits
- advanced copy DVD downloads
- invitations to the premiere or special showings
- a role in your film, such as being an extra in a crowd scene or a voice over (e.g., a scream in a horror movie)
- perks, discounts, secret recipes, coupons, and tours donated from the local community (which might be

especially apropos if your community is like a character in your film)

• personal thank you-notes.

Set the price of your perks based on what might be an appropriate price for that item, keeping in mind the value of that type of perk, such as if it's something that might later have a retail price or is something special, and your own cost to fulfill it. Offer a range of perks at different values, especially at lower amounts, since 90% of the contributions are under $100. Having many smaller investors helps to give your campaign momentum, which expands your network and builds broader interest that helps to draw in the bigger investors; as your campaign builds momentum, you'll get more of both.

Set the price for items that will be sold later, such as DVDs or downloads of your film, for about the same price as they will be sold for later; you could set the price above market value, but it's probably best not to set the price too much higher, unless you are adding something of value to it, such as including a photo from the set or personal message on a video clip. Also, consider the cost of fulfillment when you offer a perk, especially at the low pricing levels under $50, to be sure the fulfillment cost matches your effort to fulfill the item. Be sure to fulfill your perks if your campaign is successful.

To share your campaign with potential funders, Indiegogo recommends many different marketing and promotional strategies:

- Tell people about your campaign before you launch it so you can start raising funds on the first day. Use all sorts of channels to promote it, from personal contacts to e-mail, social media, blogs, or your website. Then, continue to keep people engaged throughout the campaign.

- Reach out to your inner circle, including your family, closest friends, and fans. Aim for the first 25% of your goal to come from here, and then these funds will provide a marker for others to see that your campaign has some momentum, which can jumpstart your fundraising efforts.

- Send out an announcement to your Facebook social network, create a Facebook page or group for your film, or create a Facebook event as part of your campaign. Post occasional status updates on Facebook to let others know how your campaign is going, and post information about your campaign on the walls of related organizations or pages.

- Send out a Twitter blast from your personal account and create a Twitter profile for your project. Follow journalists, similar organizations, or other users who might be especially interested in what you are doing; then, contact them to try to get them to spread the word. You can also link your campaign to your Twitter profile.

- Blog about your campaign and add a campaign widget as a sidebar or make your post about the campaign sticky, so it remains on top of the blog when you add more posts. You can add a campaign banner, too.

- Use YouTube and Vimeo to post a series of videos about your campaign, and include profiles, interviews, examples of your work (such as photos from your set), and other in-depth information about what you are doing. Add a link from your campaign to these videos.

- Post photos of your campaign's progress on Flickr, even though you can't directly sell anything; also, include a campaign link.

- Include a link to your campaign in your Google Chat status message.

- Include a link to your campaign on your website (or create a website for your campaign), and add a campaign banner here, too.

- If you have an e-newsletter, include information on your campaign—and if you don't already have an e-newsletter, start one.

- Add a link to your campaign to the bottom of your e-mail signature, which is a subtle way to let others know about your campaign and a good way to reach out to others whom you may not be able to contact through Facebook, Twitter, or other social media platforms.

- Add information about your campaign and updates to any other sites where you have a profile with your bio or information about yourself, such as LinkedIn.

Promote your campaign offline, too:

- Include a campaign URL on your business card or create cards just for your campaign; hand these out to your contacts and those you meet.
- Create an attractive flyer and post them where those who might be interested in your campaign can find them.
- Send a donation letter to your mailing list, or include a note with information about your campaign with other mailings.
- Create an appealing postcard and mail it to your mailing list or distribute it around town to places with potential backers.
- Go to events related to your project—such as lectures, screenings, and meetups—and bring along your business cards, postcards, and flyers. Then, talk up your campaign or leave your literature around.
- Go to conferences and trade shows, and apart from mingling and networking, set up a table (if it fits your budget).
- Throw your own fundraiser or benefit and invite people who might be potential backers.

- Conduct a PR campaign by sending out a press release to a targeted list of media outlets (e.g., newspapers, TV, radio) in your local area.
- Get your family and close friends involved in your campaign by giving them some postcards or flyers to take to their own contacts to spread the word for you.
- If you're part of any clubs, groups, or other social networks, ask to make an announcement at the beginning or end of the meeting to let people know about your project. You can give out flyers or postcards after your announcement, too.

Posting Campaign Updates

Keeping both backers and potential backers updated about your campaign is important, too. Indiegogo recommends posting an update every 1 to 5 days to keep everyone involved in your funding progress. While you can add updates to your blog, website, social media presence, and other sources, an advantage of adding updates to your campaign site is that Indiegogo (and many other platforms) will send an e-mail to all of your backers and fans.

The major benefits of updates are that you build trust and community by showing progress, and you build your "gogo-factor" based on having more people interacting with your campaign and sharing it—and that will up your chances of your campaign being featured on Indiegogo's homepage, blogs, or newsletter, thus getting you more funds.

Getting Paid

With Indiegogo, if you have a fixed funding campaign, you'll only get paid if you reach or exceed your goal; if it's a flexible funding campaign, which most people choose, you'll get paid whatever you earn, based on the company's fee structure. While you can accept credit cards, it's best to use PayPal—and if you have tax-deductible perks, you have to use PayPal. The big advantage is the PayPal contributions go immediately to your PayPal account, and then you can withdraw them and send them to your bank; plus, you get a 5% refund on these fees if you reach your goal. With a credit card, the funds raised are held until your campaign ends and then are sent to your bank, which can take up to 2 weeks.

Managing Your Campaign

Manage your campaign and track its progress with Indiegogo's analytics program on your campaign dashboard. Among other things, you can track the amount of funds you have raised, your views, and traffic referrals (i.e., the people who found your campaign through a link on another site). Plus, you can learn which of your backers and fans have helped spread the word about your campaign. This analysis can also help show you the relationship between the number of views and visits you are getting and the number of contributions. Having many visitors and views but few contributions can be normal when a campaign is first starting, but if you notice a pattern, remind those people to contribute. If your campaign isn't doing well and hasn't raised any funds, you can always hide it and re-launch it later.

Following Up After Your Campaign

If anyone has contributed, you should post an update or send an e-mail to thank them. If possible, send a personal thank-you to each contributor, and let people know how to contact you and when they will receive their perks (ideally immediately or within a few days or weeks of your campaign ending). If there's any delay, let you contributors know; you are actually obligated to fulfill your perks under Indiegogo's terms of service.

You can continue to post updates after your campaign ends, which is an ideal way to maintain the relationships you've established with your contributors and even set the stage for a follow-up campaign. If you do a follow-up campaign, it's a good idea to use a title similar to your old one, so it's clear that it's a continuation of your first campaign. Then, in pitching your new campaign, refer and link to the old campaign, and note what the funds were used for. You might thank your past contributors, let them know what their contributions helped you do, and then describe how your new campaign will build on your first campaign.

Making Your Campaign a Success and Avoiding the Biggest Mistakes

The campaign itself is a little like producing a film, starting with a preproduction phase of getting ready. Then, setting up the campaign and using updates to follow up is a little like conducting the film shoot and edit. Afterwards you have a big period for marketing and promoting your campaign, which is much like distributing a film.

So, what can go wrong? Apart from the failure of not taking enough time to properly promote your campaign, the major mistakes that crowdfunders make are the following:

- A lack of sustained effort and follow-through. You have to plan what you'll do before you launch your campaign and continually communicate to keep the momentum going.
- A goal that's set too high. The problem with setting your goal too high is it may seem unrealistic, or as though you aren't getting the momentum for people to think it's going to happen. Generally, once you reach 30% or more, you'll be more likely to succeed. Set your goal to the minimum needed to move your project forward, and help get the momentum going by raising the first 30% from your own network of friends, family, and co-workers, since they

won't care if you don't have any funds yet. Then, getting a higher percentage of your funding will lend credibility to your campaign and lead to more contributions.

- Jumping the gun with marketing and promotion. You only have one chance to make a good first impression, so if you try marketing or promoting your campaign widely too early, you'll lack credibility. Also, the press won't respond at this early stage, because they want something newsworthy. Thus, it's critical to get momentum first by starting with those closest to you; then after you gain their support, reach out to your next circle of people. Once you have a substantial amount of funds raised (30% or 40%), you can release your announcement to the press.

- Having a dry, business-like pitch. This will be a turn-off, since your pitch should share your enthusiasm and tell a compelling story. Use visuals, too, and break up your copy with bold headers so it's easy to read. Make it personal based on knowing your audience and what appeals to them. People want to see your face, your voice, and know why this project is important to you. Also, say quickly and specifically what you'll do with the backers' money. Besides showing pictures of your project, show pictures of your perks or even a video.

- Picking perks that don't work. Getting the perks right is very important. Offer perks of varying price ranges, and keep your pricing appropriate for the perks you choose.

Physical perks are great, since people may like to have a kind of memento of your campaign.

Some Last Tips to Make Your Campaign a Success
Here are some final tips for a successful campaign:

- Don't worry about your idea being stolen. You have to put information about your idea out there, and idea theft is very rare, since it's the execution that makes an idea successful. Also, when you put your project out there, you are already far ahead of anyone who tries to copy you.
- Once people give to your campaign, they may give again if you can keep them engaged and part of your community; 60% of the successful campaigns have repeat funders.
- Keep in mind the holidays, since contributions commonly go down over the holidays. However, if something ties into a holiday, such as being a great Christmas present (e.g., a DVD of your film), promote that, but you have to be able to fulfill the offer before the holiday.

- Reach out to influential people to share your store. For example, use Facebook or LinkedIn to reach out to influencers in your industry, try posting on their wall, and ask them to re-tweet your message. Look for influential bloggers and writers and let them know what you are doing.

RocketHub

RocketHub is another popular crowdfunding platform that uses much the same model as Indiegogo, where you get everything you collect—except if you reach your goal, you only pay a 4% fee, plus 4% for credit card processing, whereas if you don't, you pay 8%, plus the 4% processing fee. It's called the "All & More" system.

As with Kickstarter and Indiegogo, you (the "Creative") set a financial goal and time limit (between 15 and 90 days) that can't be changed, and you offer a series of rewards of different values. While RocketHub similarly talks about reaching out to your close circle first and then expanding outward, the company distinguishes between three types of backers, called "fuelers," who include the following:

- The Committed, who are "devoted to supporting an Individual Creative." They are commonly pre-existing friends and family who "will support the Creative every time, regardless of the project."
- The Inspired, who watch the project video or read the project description and, based on that, "decide that the Creative is up to something great!" They are not initially committed to fueling when they first read about the project, but they are inspired to contribute by the Creative.
- The Shoppers, who are "primarily interested in a specific reward."

RocketHub explains how to create your strategy through its "Crowdfunding Manifesto," and shares tactics through its "Crowdfunding Toolkit." It also suggests a series of "difficulty levels" based on how much you are seeking for your project and how many contributors you need to get there. The manifesto in particular provides a novel and simple way of thinking about the three equally important major elements, or "pillars," of success: the project, the network, and the rewards.

- The qualities that go into a great RocketHub project are similar to what Kickstarter and Indiegogo recommend. You should have passion, create an emotional connection with your audience, and describe why your project is important to you.
- Your first-degree network is your family and friends, who are usually the first contributors because they already trust you. Next comes your second-degree network, which includes friends of friends and acquaintances, who join once they see enough money already in the bank (e.g., about 30% to 40% of the total funds needed). For a large project, you also need your third-degree network—people who are not personally connected to you—who are the largest and most financially powerful group to fully reach your goal. It takes a lot of work to win your third-degree network's trust, and therefore

their money, so be sure your project inspires a growing momentum.

• Your rewards menu is what entices people to contribute based on your items offered at various price points. In effect, you use these different price points to effectively monetize your network by enabling people to participate based on their financial means, as well as the appeal of the items you are offering in various categories.

RocketHub provides a list of eight steps to a successful campaign:

1. Commit to the campaign by uploading a project that is built on the key principles of the manifesto and toolkit.

2. Reach out to your "first followers," which include your 15 to 25 "loyalists" (your family, friends, and fans who trust you).

3. Thank "first followers" publicly, such as on your project page and through Facebook, Twitter, and anywhere else you can show others your gratitude.

4. Expand your project out to your social network, such as announcing it on your e-mail list and on the various social media sites. Keep your tone fun and

entertaining, emphasizing how you are offering a "fun
journey and real value."

5. Keep the story going by regularly updating your proj-
    ect page, such as with blog posts and comments and by
    changing your video or adding new ones. Also, bring
    attention your accomplishments and upcoming mile-
    stones, such as achieving a certain number of backers
    or percentage of funding, or getting mentioned on a
    blog or in the press.

6. Keep people talking about your campaign by find-
    ing new ways to stay relevant and get your followers
    returning, such as for new information, rewards, and
    fun events.

7. Reach out to the press once your project has mo-
    mentum.

8. Repeat steps 3 to 7 until the last few days of your cam-
    paign, when you should end your campaign strong,
    sending out more frequent short messages. In these,
    express both the urgency of getting more contribu-
    tions and your gratitude for this support. Finally,
    thank everyone for joining you.

If you reach your goal (or at least come close), acknowledge, publicize, and gratefully celebrate that you have reached it. Also, keep your backers updated on what you are doing, let them know when you are delivering your rewards, invite their further input, and then deliver the rewards you promised. In fact, ask your backers to share their reactions, which can help you broaden your audience, so you can be even more successful in your next crowdfunding project.

Summing Up: How to Have a Successful Crowdfunding Campaign

The basic principles of having a successful crowdfunding campaign apply regardless of what platform you use, and it's a good idea to choose only one platform at a time so you don't diffuse and confuse your audience with different campaigns and make it harder to reach your goal. Perhaps it might be a good idea to use a different platform if a previous campaign didn't worked, because of the transparency principle where potential backers may be able to see if you've had previous campaigns that didn't make it or got canceled before you achieved your goal—but don't use them simultaneously.

The basic principle is to have a clearly stated goal for your project, use a catchy title, and support it with a strong description of who you are, what you plan to do, why you need the money, and what you'll use it for. Use at least one video to illustrate what you are doing, add in plenty of visuals, and make your campaign seem fun and exciting.

Have a realistic goal, and if it's too big, divide it up into parts, and then build future campaigns on previous ones. Also, select a series of rewards of different values ranging from small (under $10) to medium-size and larger goals, and combine this pricing with rewards that are appropriately priced. Stick to around the retail price or a little higher for items that can be purchased; use digital downloads, thank-yous, or easy-to-provide rewards for the lower levels; and offer special or limited-quantity higher-priced awards, which might include executive producer credits, visits to your set, or opportunities to actively participate in the project in some way.

Then, no matter how great your initial announcement and rewards, you have to heavily market and promote your campaign so it spreads. It's a good idea to start with your immediate circle of close friends and family to raise some initial investment to help you gain credibility and momentum; figure on getting about 25% to 30% from them, and then spread out to your outer circle of business associates and contacts through social media. You should wait on reaching out to the press until you have gained this momentum; otherwise, they probably won't be interested, since they are looking for a newsworthy story—and until you show you have gained support otherwise, you simply aren't news.

You also need to provide regular updates throughout your campaign to keep people engaged and expand your reach. Once you reach your goal, you need to be able to fulfill the rewards you promised and show your appreciation as you celebrate your win.

Thus, a crowdfunding campaign is not a quick and easy way to riches, although the fabulous successes of some big winners may suggest the opposite. Rather, it takes a lot of work to market and promote the campaign, especially since the idea of crowdfunding has grown, so there's a huge amount of clutter, and only about 50% of the campaigns actually do reach their goals.

Accordingly, if you are planning a crowdfunding campaign, do extensive planning in advance, not only what you'll post to feature your campaign on a crowdfunding platform, but also how you'll continually market, promote, and update it. Then, plan to spend at least 2 or 3 hours a day—or hire an assistant—to keep your campaign updated and to promote it. You may find you have to spend as much time organizing and promoting your crowdfunding campaign as you do preparing to shoot your film, so be prepared to put in the effort—or don't do it. You may have a great film project and great online posting about your campaign, but you probably won't reach your goal; you may not even

get any contributors, because you haven't done what it takes
to reach out to build credibility and trust and gain momentum, and potential backers may not have heard about you.

CHAPTER 4

Marketing, Presenting, and Promoting Your Project

Once you have laid the groundwork for getting funds for your project, the next step is finding prospective investors or contributors, presenting your project, and selling them on your idea.

Finding Prospective Investors and Contributors

One of the hardest things is actually finding the prospective investors, because even when you set up a crowdfunding campaign, you still have to reach out to people and convince them to invest in or contribute to your project. Basically, you have to sell them on your project through your promotional material, your presentation, your management team, and even yourself. The first step is finding people to approach. There are many ways to do this; use the approach that is most appropriate for you and your project.

Family and Friends

Sometimes called FAF or FOF (i.e., family and/or friends) fundraising, this is perhaps the easiest way to get started: your family and friends can help you often by simply writing a check as a gift or loan that doesn't have to be paid back if the venture goes south. In fact, many film dynasties have continued their legacy by funding their kids, such as Sophia Coppola getting a contribution from Francis Ford Coppola to get started as director. To avoid any misunderstandings, write up an agreement to indicate what you'll pay back if you're successful and what percentage in the film or film company the investor or contributor will receive going forward.

Business and Work Associates

In some professional fields, such as the tech industry, an investment in film may be an exciting departure for prospective investors and contributors who have the money. For this group, investing a small amount of discretionary funds in a film venture is much like going on a gambling jaunt to Vegas. They may like the idea of visiting the set, meeting actors, going to film festivals, and other film-related activities as a break from their ordinary routine. If so, appeal to them on that level first; give them the sizzle before you bring out the investment documents.

Doctors, Dentists, and Other High-Income Professionals

Another good prospect for new films is doctors, dentists, and other high-income professionals, such as high-end real estate brokers, who may have similar motivations to business and work associates in certain fields. However, you have to seek out ways to contact this group. One possible route is your own dentist or doctor, for example—although rather than ask for an investment directly, ask for referrals for contacts or associations in the field. Then, you may be able to contact them directly or attend an association meeting or convention to recruit these investors.

Places That Wealthy People Go

This can be a good source of investment if you interest someone in your project, because they can easily write a big check. But as one filmmaker who has found wealthy investors for his project told me, "Take some time to build a relationship first. Go to some of their events, such as an auction, art opening, or fashion show, and just hang out. Get to know someone, and then don't approach them directly. Ask if they know someone who might be interested or let them ask you for more information, since a direct approach will be a turn-off."

Film Funding Associations and Groups

Go to major film events and conferences, such as the American Film Market, held each November in Santa Monica, or

join a group on Facebook or LinkedIn (such as the Film
Financing Forum, the Film Financing Group, Hollywood
Funds, and Movie Investors Worldwide) devoted to raising
funds for films. Take some time to join the conversation, see
what people are talking about, and look for leads before
posting your own pitch. Some Meetup groups in major cities with a film community, such as L.A., San Francisco, and
New York, can also be a source of meeting or getting leads
to prospective investors. You also might attend some film
finance conferences, such as the Film Finance Forum West,
organized in association with *Variety* magazine each year.

Angel and Investor Groups

Look for angel and investor groups in your area and learn
what is needed to make a pitch to these groups, including
any charges. Then, be prepared to make a dynamic 5-min-
ute pitch, where you sell the sizzle and highlight the return
and management team, preferably with a video or Power-
Point presentation to help sell your idea.

Film Festivals

Many festivals are devoted to scripts, short films, and trailers, or have divisions within larger festivals where you can
enter your material. Some of the bigger ones also attract
investors and distributors, such as Sundance, Telluride,
Austin, and the Los Angeles Film Festival, and garnering

awards at these festivals can help you appeal to prospective investors. You can find out about these festivals at Without a Box (https://www.withoutabox.com) and iFilmfest (http://www.ifilmfestapp.com/blog).

Pitch Blasts

Send out an e-mail pitch to film producers and agents/managers, or send a pitch to casting directors and directors in order to get some letters of intent that can then be used to help you get distributors or funding—the more elements you can put together for your project, the better you will be able to interest investors. You can do this yourself if you can put together your own database from a directory, or use a service such as Publishers and Agents (http://www.publishersandagents.com), which does mailings to film producers and agents/managers, or Film and TV Connection (http://www.filmandtvconnection.com), which does mailings to others in the film industry. I work with Publishers and Agents as a writer and consultant, after having sold the company to the new owners nearly 5 years ago, and Film and TV Connection is my own company.

Have a Fundraising Party

In his book *The Fundraising Houseparty*, Morrie Warshawski recommends this basic approach: Send people an invitation to come to a party at a private home, and clearly indicate that the event is a fundraiser. Serve some refreshments and provide a brief presentation. Then, have the host or a peer stand up and invite people to make a contribution. Commonly, this kind of party raises about $3,000–$7,000, so it can supplement your other fundraising efforts, but not be the only one. The event should be in the host's home, not a restaurant, art gallery, theater, or other space, because this provides a "personal imprimatur" to you and your cause.

Presenting Your Project Online and in Person

It's important to create an online presence for your project, which can be done through multiple media outlets, including Facebook or a stand-alone site. Create a website presence for your film, such as the one created for *The Suicide Party* (http://www.suicidepartyfilm.com). If you are doing a special promotion to attract interest to your film—such as our "Save Dave" campaign, named for the film's main character, who is having a suicide party—create a website for that. At http://www.savedave.net/videos, for example, people can contribute short videos with the reasons to save Dave. On any of these kinds of sites, you can post photos of the film or the management team, as well as photos and links to film-related media.

If possible, create a sizzle reel, trailer, or short episode, or at a minimum, create a personal video where you talk about the film as you might at a formal presentation. In fact, if you do a presentation to angel investors or another group to pitch the film, arrange to have this videotaped so you can use it elsewhere, too. It's possible to do these short videos for a minimal budget if you can interest members of a local film group or film school; then, your only expenses might be for locations, props, and food for the cast and crew. Alternatively, you might hire a local film group for about $2,000–$3,000 to create a short for you, which should be immediately compelling with good cinematography and sound to best showcase your film. At the same time, you can take photos on the set, or bring in a volunteer or professional photographer to do this. It's important that any video look professional, even if it's not the final cast and crew; if the video is not of sufficient professional quality, don't show it. It's better to use a treatment or story board to illustrate the concept, because it will be difficult for prospective investors and contributors to make the leap from considering an amateur effort to imagining what a professional film shoot will be like. In some cases, trailers have been so powerful that they have led to a deal, such as the *Dead Island* trailer, which led to a movie deal in 2011 after it got 2 million views in 2 days. Another earlier example is *Panic Attack*, featuring giant robots attacking and destroying Montevideo, the capital of Uruguay, where the director received $30 million from Sam Raimi to make a sci-fi feature film after the innovative video attracted 1.5 million views.

It's best to have a sizzle reel of about 60–90 seconds or a trailer of 2–5 minutes—or both—to initially present to investors or contributors; then, if they are interested, you can show them more, such as an initial episode of about 5–10 minutes from the film. For examples, visit my You-Tube channel (http://www.youtube.com/changemakers-prod), which includes sizzle reels and videos from a crime film, *The Parking Lot* (script trailer: http://www.youtube.com/watch?v=0QEEWmMX8wk; sizzle reel: http://www.youtube.com/watch?v=iUalPgJmPTA) and from a sci-fi feature, *Dead No More* (script trailer: http://www.youtube.com/watch?v=dG057_926l0; sizzle reel: http://www.youtube.com/watch?v=zx-nanJqFRE).

Promoting Your Project Through Traditional and Social Media

The more you can get noticed by the media, the more you up your chances of getting funds for your film. This promotion can take several forms:

1. getting promotion for yourself, featuring your professional careers

2. getting promotion for your company, highlighting what your company has done in creating shorts, videos, and other projects in the film industry

3. getting promotion for your proposed film project, including any book, story, or person it's based on; or

4. a combination of these.

You can do what you can yourself, perhaps using a guide such as *The Complete Guide to Doing Your Own PR*, which I wrote to help you. Or hire a PR individual or firm to help you navigate both traditional and social media, since they will have already developed contacts and will commonly use a subscription service, such as Cision, which provides access to a continually updated database of media contacts.

The traditional approach involves getting featured in traditional media, including newspapers, magazines, radio, TV, and Internet publications and broadcasts. Commonly, these outlets are contacted through press releases, along with phone calls before sending the release to alert them to it or afterwards to follow up. In some cases, you might target a small number of editors or show producers who might be especially interested in your project before you widely distribute your release. There are also assorted PR services that will send out releases for you, such as PRWire, BusinessWire, PRWeb, PRBuzz, and ExpertClick.

In sending out these releases, it's helpful to have a tie-in to something going on in the news, rather than simply promoting plans for a future film project. For example, if your film relates to a current incident or social trend, mention that in your release.

With social media, you might create a campaign where you send out regular updates on Twitter, Facebook, LinkedIn, Reddit, and other popular social networking sites. Such a campaign might be linked to a page you set up for the film on Facebook, a film website, videos on YouTube or Vimeo, or a crowdfunding campaign on Kickstarter, RocketHub, or Indiegogo. Then, set a goal of increasing the number of likes, fans, or friends, since your greater popularity will help you attract interest from prospective investors and contributors. Expect to spend at least 2 hours a day building this promotion—or hire one of the many social media firms or specialists to help you mount your campaign.

CHAPTER 5

Closing the Deal and Getting Your Funds

Closing the Deal

With a crowdfunding campaign, contributors simply make their contributions online, and you fulfill any rewards you have promised after you get your funds or complete the film.

In the case of investors, you'll need to follow-up with discussions, e-mails, and negotiations, depending on the nature of the deal you are proposing and any counteroffers prospects make to you. The specifics of this process are too varied to discuss here, but in general, be prepared to be flexible, especially with larger investors, and provide them with an agreement detailing the terms of the deal—such as how much they are investing and how and when they will get their money back (such as getting the first moneys out after the film makes money until they get their original investment back with interest, and then get a percentage share of the additional earnings—commonly a percentage of the 45% to 50% investors' share, based on the size of their investment and the total amount invested). Then, you both sign the agreement.

In some cases, you may find that a prospective investor proposes an alternate deal, because he or she wants to produce, direct, act, or otherwise play a larger role in your film project. Then, depending on how committed you are to your current management team and any crew and cast who want to participate, you might consider changing your original arrangements. For example, you may envision getting $100,000 to produce the film locally with a selected director and DP, and with many of the crew and cast who are still interested and available from the short and sizzle reel you created. But then an investor envisions a $1 million budget, working with a director and DP he has worked with before and filming in another city, with you as an assistant director or second camera. Or maybe an investor/producer simply wants to buy your script. In such a case, assess what is most important to you, along with the likelihood of getting the funds you need to produce the film yourself. These situations may be a good way of gaining additional credibility and experience to find funds for your next film—or you may want to continue seeking the funds to produce your film on a smaller scale, and use this experience to help you get funding for your next project.

Getting Your Money and Disbursing Your Funds

Finally, once you do get your money, have a bank account set up for your film—commonly as a separate LLC or as a separate account within your company—so you can keep track of the funds you receive and disburse for your film. Work with an accountant or bookkeeper, or use an accounting program such as QuickBooks to keep track of everything you spend. In some cases, you can use this accounting to apply for incentives, such as getting your payments for certain locations back from the city or federal government after you complete your film.

Now, go get your money! And best of luck in making your film.

Appendix

Example: Log Lines for *The Suicide Party*

60 words; 360 characters: A ripped-from-the headlines drama about a formerly successful business professional who can't find work, is losing his house, and decides to throw a suicide party with his friends' help to raise money to get back on his feet. If he raises enough he'll live; otherwise he'll kill himself; putting on the party leads to a media frenzy and unexpected results.

25 words; 140 characters: A businessman losing it all throws a suicide party with friends; if he raises enough he'll live; if not he won't, with unexpected results.

Example: Synopsis for *The Suicide Party*

500 words; 2,800 characters: It starts with a brief introduction, followed by 2 paragraphs about the story and then a brief introduction to the screenplay writer. Or make it even shorter: say 300–400 words and 2000 characters if so requested. In any case, it should be single spaced

and fit on one page. Although you might write a synopsis for audience members that leaves the ending of the story hanging, because you want audience members to go see the movie, most distributors, sales reps, and investors want to know how things turn out—so include most of the plot highlights in your synopsis (but you can leave out a twist that occurs at the end).

Sample: Letter of Intent for *The Parking Lot*

This letter of intent from an actor was used in developing and pitching *The Parking Lot* (names have been changed).

LETTER OF INTENT FOR ATTACHMENT
JANE JONES, SAG

JANE JONES, SAG has read the script entitled THE PARKING LOT by Gini Graham Scott, and is interested in playing the lead antagonist role of Maureen in the aforementioned feature film, subject to terms and conditions providing the funding of the project.

Jessica Fox, creative producer for the entitled project, intends to use Jane Jones's bio and reel for submission to third parties.

My participation in this project is based on my professional availability and good faith negotiations.

All the best,
Jane Jones, SAG

Sample: Letter of Intent for *The Parking Lot*

This letter of intent is for a director for *The Parking Lot* (names have been changed).

LETTER OF INTENT FOR ATTACHMENT
DANIEL SMITH

I have read the screenplay entitled THE PARKING LOT, written by Gini Graham Scott, and would be pleased to direct this feature film project, subject to the approval of your financiers. From a director's viewpoint, I believe the story to be well written and could see it being a commercially successful film.

I hereby give permission to Jessica Fox, the creative producer of the project, to use my reel, as is customary in the film and television industry, to assist in the securing of financing, distribution, and/or lead actors. This permission shall continue until I give written notice to the contrary.

As always, my participation in the project will be subject to my availability and to mutually acceptable terms with respect to my compensation and subject to all requirements of the DGA.

Yours truly,
Daniel Smith

Chart: Organizational Structures

Type of Structure	Type of Funding				
	Family & Friends	1-2 wealthy Investors	Angel Investors	Venture Capitalists	Share Holders
Sole Proprietorship	X	X			
General Partnership	X	X			
Joint Venture	X	X	X	X	
Initial Incorporation	X	X	X	X	
Member-Managed LLC	X	X	X	X	
Manager-Managed LLC	X	X	X	X	
Limited Partnership	X	X	X	X	
C-Corporation	X	X	X	X	X
S-Corporation	X	X	X	X	X

Example: Shooting Schedule for *Actor*

This shooting schedule was prepared for one of Changemakers Productions' clients for a film called *Actor* that was budgeted at about $1.5 million, based on a shoot of 24 days with largely unknown actors. Later, after client believed he could get some name actors, the length of the shoot was expanded and the budget increased to $5 million based on the higher salaries paid to these stars. So the scheduler and budget preparer adjusted the documents accordingly, although more realistically the budget was about $1.5 million based on the original schedule and more realistic plans for the shoot.

"ACTOR"
Shooting Schedule

Shoot Day # 1 Monday, July 9, 2012

EXT	PATH BY THE	Day	**Cast Members**
Scene # 11		1 5/8 Pgs	1 TIMOTHY
			16 ALEX

Timothy runs into a hoodlum that offers a hiest

COMMENTS:

EXT	PARK NEAR SCHOOL	Day	**Cast Members**
Scene # 14		1 4/8 Pgs	1 TIMOTHY
			3 JESSICA

talking about the short they will do

| | | | 4 JONATHAN |
| | | | 17 MICHELE |

COMMENTS:

End Day # 1 Monday, July 9, 2012 -- Total Pages: 3 1/8

Shoot Day # 2 Tuesday, July 10, 2012

EXT	CITY PARK	Day	**Cast Members**
Scene # 57		3 2/8 Pgs	1 TIMOTHY
			3 JESSICA

doing their short film

			4 JONATHAN
			23 STUDENT DIRECTOR
			24 STUDENT SCRIPT SUPERVISOR
			Background Actors students

COMMENTS:

EXT	CITY PARK	Day	**Cast Members**
Scene # 58		1 5/8 Pgs	1 TIMOTHY
			3 JESSICA

Timothy & Jessica get into heavy kissing

			4 JONATHAN
			23 STUDENT DIRECTOR
			24 STUDENT SCRIPT SUPERVISOR

Printed on Feb 9, 2012 at 1:48 PM   Page 1
(Continued on next page)

Example: Budget for *Actor*

The budget created for *Actor* was based on the client's request to make this a $5 million budget, although without name actors and a shorter shoot, as originally projected, it could have been a $1.5 million shoot. The first 2 pages are the summary, or "top sheet," which is usually included in a business plan or producer package, while the rest of the plan is in the appendix or available on request. A first page of the detailed budget is also included as an example. Note that the budget is divided into above-the-line and below-the-line (i.e., Production, Post-Production, and Other) sections.

"ACTOR"
Feature Film Production Budget

Producers:Richard Murphy, Lester Augustine III
Budget by: Gary A. Lowe (818-509-7910)
Prepared: Feb 20. 2012 REV Mar1
Based on Schedule from 109 pg script

Unions: SAG. IA .Teamster. DGA
Schedule: 5 weeks, 25 days
Location: Glendale. CA
Format: HD RED Epic
Director: Alton Glass

Acct#	Category Description	Page	Total
1100	STORY, RIGHTS & CONTINUITY	1	$170,500
1200	PRODUCERS UNIT	1	$289,242
1300	DIRECTION	2	$372,750
1400	CAST	2	$761,261
1500	TRAVELING & LIVING COSTS	4	$36,050
	Total Above-The-Line		**$1,629,803**
2000	PRODUCTION STAFF	6	$333,305
2100	EXTRA TALENT	8	$207,799
2200	SET DESIGN	9	$85,960
2300	MECHANICAL FX	10	$9,800
2500	SET OPERATIONS	10	$172,820
2700	SET DRESSING	12	$150,842
2800	PROPERTY	13	$70,561
2900	WARDROBE	14	$138,883
3100	MAKEUP & HAIR	16	$98,266
3200	LIGHTING	17	$144,237
3300	CAMERA	18	$114,679
3400	PRODUCTION SOUND	19	$46,617
3500	TRANSPORTATION	20	$324,027
3600	LOCATION	22	$228,110
4300	FRINGE BENEFITS & PYRLL TAXES	23	$0
	Total Production		**$2,125,905**
4200	POST PRODUCTION	24	$65,645
4500	EDITING	25	$115,664
4600	MUSIC	26	$150,268
4700	POST PRODUCTION SOUND	27	$40,000
4900	MAIN & END TITLES	27	$10,100
	Total Post Production		**$381,677**
6500	PUBLICITY	29	$36,000
6600	PUBLICITY - RESEARCH SCREENING	29	$10,000
6700	INSURANCE	29	$93,000
6800	GENERAL EXPENSE	29	$51,200
6900	FINANCE	31	$260,000
	Total Other		**$450,200**
	Contingency : 10 0%		$458,759

The Entertainment Partners Services Group, MM Budgeting

Acct#	Category Description	Page	Total
	Completion Bond : 3.5%		$160,566
	Total Above-The-Line		**$1,629,803**
	Total Below-The-Line		**$2,957,782**
	Total Above and Below-The-Line		**$4,587,586**
	Grand Total		**$5,206,910**

ACTOR   Page 1

Acct#	Description	Amt	Units	X	Rate	Sub T	Total
1100 STORY, RIGHTS & CONTINUITY							
1101	Writers						
	Screenplay	1	Allow	1	150,000	150,000	
	Polish	1	Allow	1	10,000	10,000	
	Total						$160,000
1102	Rights purchased						$0
1103	Story consult, editors & analyst						$0
1104	Clearances						
	Research/Clearances	1	Allow	1	5,000	5,000	
	E & O legal	1	Allow	1	2,500	2,500	
	Total						$7,500
1105	Copying						
	Script	1	Allow	1	500	500	
	Total						$500
1107	Secretaries						$0
1185	Other costs - living & travel						
	to Location	1	Allow	1	2,500	2,500	
	Total						$2,500
1195	Studio charges						$0
1199	Fringe benefits & payroll taxes						$0
	Total Fringes						$0
Account Total for 1100							**$170,500**
1200 PRODUCERS UNIT							
1201	Producers						
	Producer #1	1	Allow	1	100,000	100,000	
	Producer #2	1	Allow	1	100,000	100,000	
	Total						$200,000
1204	Line Producer						
	Prep	8	Weeks	1	4,000	32,000	
	Shoot	5	Weeks	1	4,000	20,000	
	Wrap	1	Week	1	4,000	4,000	
	Total						$56,000
1207	Secretaries						
	for Producers	12	Weeks	1	800	9,600	
	Total						$9,600
1208	Legal & Audit						
	Contracts (Legal)	1	Allow	1	15,000	15,000	
	Total						$15,000
1210	Development Costs						$0

Resource: Comparable Films

When creating your financial plan, you can take the following films in the last 10 years with low budgets to illustrate what is possible and then look for data on comparable films in your genre and budget.

Source: The Numbers, http://www.the-numbers.com/movies/

Release Date	Movie	Distributor	Budget	Worldwide Gross	Percent Return
9/25/2009	*Paranormal Activity*		$15,000	$196,681,656	655,505.52%
5/7/2004	*Super Size Me*	IDP/Sam Goldwyn	$65,000	$29,529,368	22,614.90%
5/16/2007	*Once*	Fox Searchlight	$150,000	$18,997,174	6,232.39%
6/11/2004	*Napoleon Dynamite*	Fox Searchlight	$400,000	$46,140,956	5,667.62%

Sample: Comparable Films Table

Potential Profits Based on a Comparison of Grosses and Costs of Comparable Films						
	Pict 1	Pict 2	Pict 3	Pict 4	Pict 5	Average
Total Producer's Gross						
Less Production Cost of **Comparables**						
Net Investor/Producer Profits						
Total Gross						
Less Production Cost of **Your** Film						
Net Investor/Producer Profits						

Sample: Projected Cash Flow Table

Projected Cash Flow Based on Moderate Profit Projections (Millions of Dollars)												
	Year 1				Year 2				Year 3			
Films	Qtr 1	Qtr 2	Qtr 3	Qtr 4	Qtr 1	Qtr 2	Qtr 3	Qtr 4	Qtr 1	Qtr 2	Qtr 3	Qtr 4
Film 1												
Film 2												
Total Cash												
Cumulative Cash Flow												

Sample: Private Placement Memorandum

The following PPM was created for Changemakers Productions, based on offering up to 74 shares (the number allowed for an offering to private investors that doesn't require SEC registration) to obtain $50,000 from investors, with the producer retaining 37 shares (or 50%), so each share to investors is valued at $1,351 (37 x $1,351 = approximately $50,000). The PPM was created using the RocketLawyer online service. You can similarly create such a document for yourself by answering the key interview questions; then, have them reviewed by a lawyer in your state to be sure they meet the appropriate legal requirements.

Confidential Private Placement Memorandum
Changemakers Productions
Up to 74 shares of Common Stock at $1,351.00 per share
Maximum Offering – 74 Shares
Minimum Offering – 58 Shares
Minimum Purchase per Investor – 1 Share
This Confidential Private Placement Memorandum (the "Memorandum") has been prepared in connection with an offering (the "Offering") of up to 74 Shares of Common Stock, $1,351.00 par value (the "Shares") of Changemakers Productions (the "Company"). The minimum offering amount is 22 ("Minimum Offering Amount"), and the

maximum offering amount is 74 ("Maximum Offering Amount"). The minimum purchase per investor is 1 share, or $1,351.00. Officers and directors of the Company will make offers and sales of the Shares; however, the Company retains the right to utilize any broker-dealers registered with the National Association of Securities Dealers, Inc. ("NASD") and applicable state securities authorities to sell all or any portion of the Shares. If the Company so elects, it may pay such broker-dealers a commission in the amount of up to 10% and a non-accountable expense allowance of up to 3% of the proceeds they have sold. Offers and sales of the Shares will be made only to "Accredited Investors" as such term is defined in Rule 501 of Regulation D promulgated under the Securities Act of 1933, as amended (the "Act"), which includes the Company's officers, directors, and affiliates.

The Offering is scheduled to terminate on December 31, 2012. The Company reserves the right, however, to extend the term of this Offering for a period of up to 30 days. See "The Offering." This Memorandum may not be reproduced in whole or in part without the express prior written consent of the Company.

The date of this Confidential Private Placement Memorandum is December 01, 2012.

THIS MEMORANDUM IS FOR CONFIDENTIAL USE AND MAY NOT BE REPRODUCED [This is then followed by assorted legal boilerplate about registration and the securities being highly speculative and subject to various conditions].

EXECUTIVE SUMMARY
1. THE OFFERING
[This section includes information on how much the company plans to raise, the intended use, the rights of shareholders to vote, the shares held by the producer and other officers and employees, and the arrangements for paying dividends.]

2. BUSINESS PLAN
[This briefly describes the company's mission and marketing strategy.]

3. MANAGEMENT
[This section includes a table listing the current management, arrangements under which the directors will hold office, the possible creation of an Executive Advisory Board, and arrangements for indemnification and insurance of the directors and officers of the company.]

4. HISTORICAL FINANCIAL INFORMATION

[This section offers to provide a detailed financial history of the business on request for the previous 3 years.]

5. RISK FACTORS

[This section includes a description of the various risk factors, much of this boilerplate, which include:

- unanticipated obstacles to the execution of the business plan;
- competition;
- over-reliance on management; and
- forward-looking statements.]

ADDITIONAL INFORMATION

[This section invites prospective investors and their advisors to review any materials available about the Company, plan of operation, management, and financial condition. It restates the risk of investment, making it suitable only for persons of adequate financial means, and describes the suitability standards for making an investment as an "accredited investor."]

Resources

Copyright and Registration

US Copyright Office (http://www.copyright.gov/eco)

Writers Guild of America Registry (http://www.wgawregistry.org/webrss)

Crowdfunding

CircleUp (https://circleup.com)

Crowdfunder (http://www.crowdfunder.com)

CrowdFunding Intermediary Regulatory Advocates (http://www.cfira.org)

Crowdfunding Professional Association (CfPA) (http://www.cfpa.org)

Indiegogo (http://www.indiegogo.com)

Kickstarter (http://www.kickstarter.com)

National Crowdfunding Association (http://www.nlcfa.org)

RocketHub (http://www.rockethub.com/)

Music

ccMixter (http://ccmixter.org)

Free Music Archive (http://freemusicarchive.org)

Pond5 (http://www.pond5.com)

SoundCloud (https://soundcloud.com)

Vimeo Music Store (http://vimeo.com/musicstore)

Research Tools

Association of Film Commissioners International (http://www.afci.org)

Baseline Studio System (http://www.baselineresearch.com; http://www.studiosystem.com)

Box Office Mojo (http://www.boxofficemojo.com)

California Film Commission (http://www.film.ca.gov)

Entertainment Partners (http://www.entertainmentpartners.com/)

Film and TV Connection (http://www.filmandtvconnection.com)

The Hollywood Reporter (http://www.hollywoodreporter.com/)

iFilmfest (http://www.ifilmfestapp.com/blog)

Internet Movie Database (IMDb) (http://www.imdb.com)

Megadox (http://www.megadox.com/)

Michael Wiese Film School (http://www.mwp.com/filmschool)

Motion Picture Association of America (http://www.mpaa.org/)

Publishers and Agents (http://www.publishersandagents.com)

Nash Information Services (http://nashinfoservices.com/)

The Numbers (http://www.the-numbers.com)

Variety (http://variety.com/)

Without A Box (http://www.withoutabox.com)

Bibliography

Alberstat, Philip. 2004. *The Insider's Guide to Film Finance*. Burlington, MA: Focal Press / Elsevier.

Baddour, Nic. 2011. "Where to Price Our Perks." *Indiegogo Insight* (blog), October 20. http://blog.indiegogo.com/2011/10/where-to-price-your-perks.html.

Brew, Simon. 2012. "Does Crowdfunding Work?" PC Pro, September 28. http://www.pcpro.co.uk/features/377242/does-crowdfunding-work.

Cieply, Michael. 2012. "Hollywood Seeks to Slow Cultural Shift to TV." *New York Times*, October 28. http://www.nytimes.com/2012/10/29/movies/hollywood-seeks-to-slow-cultural-shift-to-tv.html.

"Cinema of the United States." 2013. *Wikipedia*. Last modified June 17. http://en.wikipedia.org/wiki/Cinema_of_the_United_States.

Cones, John W. 2008. *43 Ways to Finance Your Feature Film*. Carbondale: Southern Illinois University Press.

"Contents of a Written Business Plan." 2013. Find Law. Accessed July 3. http://smallbusiness.findlaw.com/starting-a-business/contents-of-a-written-business-plan.html.

"Crowd funding." 2013. *Wikipedia*. Last modified June 15. http://en.wikipedia.org/wiki/Crowd_funding.

"Crowdfunding? Know the Good and Bad." 2012. Crowdfunding Bank, October 25. http://crowdfundingbank.com/good-and-bad-funding

"Crowdfunding Tips for Campaigners." 2013. Indiegogo. Accessed July 1. http://www.indiegogo.com/crowdfunding-tips.

Davies, Adam P., and Nicol Wistreich. 2007. *The Film Finance Handbook: How to Fund Your Film*. London: Netribution.

Dean, Carole Lee. 2012. *The Art of Film Funding: Alternative Funding Concepts*. 2nd ed. Studio City, CA: Michael Wiese Productions.

"Domestic Movie Theatrical Market Summary 1995 to 2013." 2013. The Numbers, June 19. http://www.the-numbers.com/market/.

Duggan, John. 2013. "5 Box Office Predictions for 2010." *Scene Clips* (blog). January 21, 2013. http://blog.sceneclips.com/film-investing/2010-box-office-trends (site discontinued).

"Fahrenheit 9/11." 2013. *Wikipedia*. Last modified May 26. http://en.wikipedia.org/wiki/Fahrenheit_9/11.

Film Budgets. 2010. "Film Budgets: Section 181 Federal Film Tax Incentive Renewed." *Film Budget, Inc.* (blog), December 22. http://www.filmbudget.com/blog/film-budgets-section-181-federal-film-tax-incentive-renewed.

Fleishman, Glenn. 2012. "Crowdfunding: A Guide to Crowdfunding." BoingBoing, July 9. http://boingboing.net/2012/07/09/crowdfunding-a-guide-to-crowdf.html.

Global Picture Studios. 2013. "Locking in Letters of Intent for Cast." LinkedIn. Accessed July 3. http://www.linkedin.com/company/global-pictures-studios/-locking-in-letters-of-intent-for-cast-367321/product.

GoGoCatherine. 2011a. "Great Perk Ideas." Indiegogo, October 24. http://support.indiegogo.com/entries/20582388-Great-Perk-Ideas.

———. 2011b. "How to Share Your Campaign." Indiegogo, October 23. http://support.indiegogo.com/entries/20582313-How-to-Share-Your-Campaign.

Greenfield, Richard, and Brandon Ross. 2012. "Movie Industry Must Bring the Theater 'Home.'" *The Future of Film* (blog), April 15. http://tribecafilm.com/future-of-film/5136196c1c7d769461000007-movie-industry-must-bring.

Hall, Peter. 2011. "AMC and Regal Plan to Acquire and Distribute Their Own Movies." Moviefone, February 11. http://news.moviefone.com/2011/02/11/amc-regal-movie-distribution/.

"How Much Will It Cost to Form and Operate an LLC?" LegalZoom. July 3, 2013. http://www.legalzoom.com/llc-faq/llc-operating-costs.html.

"The Independent Producers and the *Paramount* Case, 1938–1949." Hollywood Renegades Archives. July 3, 2013. http://www.cobbles.com/simpp_archive/paramountcase_1slump1938.htm.

Juuso, Jeremy. 2009. *Getting the Money: A Step-by-Step Guide for Writing Business Plans for Film*. Studio City, CA: Michael Wiese Productions.

Katherine. 2010a. "10 Places to Promote Your Indiegogo Project Online." Indiegogo, September 7. http://blog.indiegogo.com/2010/09/10-places-to-promote-your-indiegogo-project-online.html.

———. 2010b. "10 Ways to Promote Your Indiegogo Project OFF-Line." Indiegogo, September 13. http://blog.indiegogo.com/2010/09/10-ways-to-promote-your-indiegogo-project-off-line.html.

———. 2011. "8 Ways to Drive Traffic to Your Campaign with Social Media." Indiegogo, May 11. http://blog.indiegogo.com/2011/05/driving-traffic-to-your-campaign-with-social-media.html.

"Kickstarter School." Kickstarter. July 3, 2013. http://www.kickstarter.com/help/school.

Koestsier, John. 2013. "Equity Crowdfunding by Unaccredited Investors Is Legal in Exactly One Place in North America." http://venturebeat.com.May 29. http://venturebeat.com/2013/05/29/crowdfunding-for-equity-by-unaccreditedinvestors-is-legal-in-exactly-one-place-innorth-america/

Knoblock, Carl. 2012. "Before Jumping In, Understand How Online Crowdfunding Works." *Pittsburgh Business Times*, July 20. http://www.bizjournals.com/pittsburgh/print-edition/2012/07/20/understand-how-online-crowdfunding-works.html.

Laurence, Beth. "How to Form a Corporation." Nolo. http://www.nolo.com/legal-encyclopedia/form-corporation-how-to-incorporate-30030.html.

Levison, Louise. 2010. *Financing: Business Plans for Independents*. Burlington, MA: Focal Press / Elsevier.

"Major Film Studio." 2013. *Wikipedia*. Last modified June 20. http://en.wikipedia.org/wiki/Major_film_studio.

"Michael Moore." 2013. *Wikipedia*. Last modified June 7. http://en.wikipedia.org/wiki/Michael_Moore.

Motion Picture Association of America. 2011. *Theatrical Market Statistics 2011*. http://www.mpaa.org/resources/5bec4ac9-a95e-443b-987b-bff6fb5455a9.pdf.

Neiss, Sherwood, Jason W. Best, and Zak Cassady-Dorion. 2013. *Crowdfund Investing For Dummies®*. Hoboken, NJ: John Wiley & Sons.

Olsson, Linus. 2011. "Crowdfunding: Get Paid for Free Stuff." *NetMagazine*, August 26. http://www.netmagazine.com/features/crowdfunding-get-paid-free-stuff.

"Private Place Memorandum Interview." RocketLawyer. http://www.rocketlawyer.com/document/private-placement-memorandum.rl

"Production Incentives Update." 2012. Directors Guide of America, March 12. http://www.dga.org/News/Guild-News/2012/April-2012/Production-Incentives-Update.aspx.

Protalinski, Emil. 2012. "Irony at Its Finest: Kickstarter Project Explaining How to Fund Kickstarter Projects Fails." *The Next Web*, September 30. http://thenextweb.com/entrepreneur/2012/09/30/irony-finest-kickstarter-project-explaining-fund-kickstarter-projects-fails.

Sandlund, Jonathan. 2012. "Enough with the Rhetoric, Crowdfunding Works—Here's the Proof." *Venture Beat*, October 12. http://venturebeat.com/2012/10/20/crowdfunding-works-heres-the-proof.

Sandy. 2011a. "Send Campaign Updates." Indiegogo, September 29. http://support.indiegogo.com/entries/20491883-Send-Campaign-Updates.

———. 2011b. "Track Your Campaign Progress with Analytics." Indiegogo, September 29. http://support.indiegogo.com/entries/20491853-Track-Your-Campaign-Progress-with-Analytics.

———. 2011c. "Relaunching a Campaign." Indiegogo, October 2. http://support.indiegogo.com/entries/20501666-Relaunching-a-Campaign.

"Statutory Damages for Copyright Infringement." 2013. Wikipedia. Last modified January 18. http://en.wikipedia.org/wiki/Statutory_damages_for_copyright_infringement.

Sullivan, Michael. 2012. "Welcome to the Crowdfunding Wiki." PBworks, December 4. http://crowdfunding.pbworks.com/w/page/10402176/Crowdfunding.

Warshawski, Morrie. 2007. The Fundraising Houseparty: How to Party with a Purpose and Raise Money for Your Cause. Ann Arbor, MI: Murdock Advertising and Design.

Writers Guild of America, West (WGAW). 2013. "WGAW Independent Film." Writers Guild of America, West. http://wga.org/subpage_writersresources.aspx?id=924.

———. 2013. Schedule of Minimums, 2011 Theatrical and Television Basic Agreement. http://www.wga.org/uploadedfiles/writers_resources/contracts/min2011.pdf.

Zimmerman, Kate. 2011a. "Create a Great Pitch." Indiegogo, August 9. http://support.indiegogo.com/entries/20353061-how-to-create-a-great-pitch.

———. 2011b. "Deleting a Campaign." Indiegogo, September 1. http://support.indiegogo.com/entries/20407982-Deleting-a-Campaign.

———. 2012a. "Choose Your Goal and Deadline." Indiegogo, Feb. 15. http://support.indiegogo.com/entries/21004972-how-to-choose-your-goal-and-deadline.

———. 2012b. "What You Can & Can't Offer as Perks." Indiegogo, February 15. http://support.indiegogo.com/entries/21012318-what-you-can-t-offer-as-perks.